Union River

Union River

Poems and Sketches

Paul Marion

Bootstrap Press
2017

Cover design by Ryan Gallagher
Author photo by Kevin Harkins

Bootstrap Press books are designed and edited by Derek Fenner and Ryan Gallagher.

East Coast:

31 Wyman Street
Lowell, MA 01852

West Coast:

1502 Alice Street #8
Oakland, CA 94612

www.bootstrappress.org

Union River

Union River

Union River

Union River

Union River

Union River

ion River

n River

Also by Paul Marion

Horsefeathers & Aquarius (1976, chapbook)
Marking Fresh Ice (1977, chapbook)
Focus on a Locus: Lowell Poems (1980, chapbook)
Essays from the Lowell Conference on Industrial History
      (1981, co-editor)
Strong Place: Poems '74-'84 (1984)
Apples and Oranges (1986, chapbook)
Middle Distance (1989)
Lowell: The Story of an Industrial City (1992, contributing author)
Merrimack: A Poetry Anthology (1992, co-editor)
Vital Records: Poems from the LIRA Writing Workshop
      (1994, editor)
Hit Singles (1995, chapbook)
Generator Room (1998, co-editor)
French Class: French Canadian-American Writings on Identity,
      Culture, and Place (1999, editor and co-author)
Atop an Underwood: Early Stories and Other Writings by Jack
      Kerouac (1999, editor)
What Is the City? (2006)
Poetry Face-Off/Poésie des Series [Canada] (2008, chapbook,
      co-author)
Cut from American Cloth: An Essay (2012, chapbook)
South Common Haiku (2012, chapbook)
Mill Power: The Origin and Impact of Lowell National Historical
      Park (2014)

Acknowledgments

Many of these poems and sketches, sometimes in different versions, have appeared in books, chapbooks, journals, magazines, newspapers, anthologies, and broadsides, and on websites, compact disc, and YouTube. My thanks to the editors and publishers of the following: *Alaska Quarterly Review*; *Appalachia*; *Apples and Oranges*; *Aspect*; *The Aspect Anthology*; *Bohemian* (Japan); *The Bridge Review: Merrimack Valley Culture* (www); *Café Review*; *Carolina Quarterly*; *The Continuing Revolution: A History of Lowell, Massachusetts*; *Cut From American Cloth: An Essay*; *Entelechy International: A Journal of Contemporary Ideas*; *For a Living: The Poetry of Work*; *French Class: French Canadian-American Writings on Identity, Culture, and Place*; *French Connections: A Gathering of Franco-American Poets*; *Heartbeat of New England: An Anthology of Contemporary Nature Poems*; *Hit Singles*; *jackmagazine* (www); *The Larcom Review*; *Lives in Translation: An Anthology of Contemporary Franco-American Writings*; *Loom broadsides*; *Lowell Offering*; *Marking Fresh Ice*; *The Merrimack Literary Review*; *Middle Distance*; *Monuments and Memory: History and Representations in Lowell, Massachusetts*; *Moody Street Irregulars*; *Nexus*; *The Offering*; *Point West*; *Potato Eyes*; *Québec Kérouac Blues* (Canada); *richardhowe.com* (www); *River Muse: Tales of Lowell and the Merrimack Valley*; *River Review/Revue Rivière*; *Road Apple Review*; *Rockhurst Review*; *Salamander*; *Salmon Literary Quarterly* (Ireland); *San Fernando Poetry Journal*; *Santa Clara Review*; *Soundings East*; *Steak Haché* (Canada); *Strong Place: Poems '74-'84*; *This Time*; *UVAS: Live from the Urban Village*; *vyü*; *What Is the City?*; *Where the Road Begins*; *Yankee*; and *Zone 3*.

For all the poets and their readers

Union River

Union River

Union River

Union River

Union River

Union River

on River

River

CONTENTS

one

two

three

four

five

six

The United States themselves are essentially the greatest poem.

Walt Whitman, *Leaves of Grass*, 1855

one

CHECKING THE PROPERTY

My nine-year-old son says, "I'm going to read the 'Gettysburg Address.'"
What's the Lincoln shorthand? Freed the slaves; saved the union.
People crowd the marble steps at dusk. A sign asks for silence.
When he sees my wife lining up a shot, a guy in a straw cowboy hat
Offers to take a picture of my wife, our son, and me.
Climbing the stairs, I had caught sight of the figure behind columns,
And then lost him due to the steep ascent,
Only to come upon the sculpture again near the top,
Where visitors gaze at the huge seated president,
Whose massive square-toed boot juts out, looking as if it could kick
Jefferson Davis' football the length of the Reflecting Pool
And onto the white spike of the Washington Monument,
At late day reflecting sun on its narrow western face,
A glow-stick numeral standing for the first president,
Who set the constitutional republic in motion,
The stone blocks a different shade on the top half,
Marking a stop in work and return, a monument telling its story,
One in which protesters rolled cut stones into the drink,
In a struggle for control of the civic project,
Foreshadowing later conflicts and comings together
On this electric stretch of public land without timber or copper,
A wide open space in which to make a verb of America—
To recall and exuberate and to do democratic research-and-development
In a red clay-lined lab, crowded with evidence of an ongoing experiment,
And bearing key formulas and equations inscribed in stone.

Colorado

1.

Heat flashes over the High Plains,
Heat lightning over the dark prairie,
Hot clouds sparking,
Bumping above the sweetgrass—
Heat-light, spur-shine,
Skylight, bright-pulse, street lamp.
July-light flicking off the Front Range,
White lines in a Denver night.

2.

Along well-marked routes I found this stop
Facing the Blood of Christ Mountains,
Far shelf of white-and-dark cake
That I imagine could be seized
If only I lean out far enough
Into the expanse beyond the guardrail.
I'm here but not grounded—a fresh context,
Mid-continent, with only a map for proof.
There's something moving out there—
The whole Earth is rolling.

3.

Death is like the last piece
Of that hundred-car coal train
Being pulled by six green Rio Grande diesels
Outside of Colorado Springs.
For the longest time
It's all noise and power and motion,
And you think the line won't end—
But there's no invented engine
To make that dream come true.

CRAZY HORSE

Sculptor Korczak Ziolkowski died in 1982 at the age of 74. His work in South Dakota continues.

Old-man Boston-born sculptor out west
Asked by Indian elders 38 years back
To create a monument of great Chief Crazy Horse
Pointing southeast on a charger,
And he began,
Wore out cases of jackhammers, burnt out bulldozers,
Meantime married, had ten kids, told wife
The mountain carving was first, she second, kids number three,
And now at 70 he's still at it,
Knocking out millions of tons of rock with dynamite and sweat,
Now working, now ordering his sons to cut rock,
And it shapes up, begins to show signs of happening,
This enormous figure, so big
He could fit Mount Rushmore's quartet in the red warrior's armpit,
So big he knows he won't polish the miles of surface,
But the veteran who helped chisel Rushmore says,
"Let me have six, seven more years,
And people coming up that road that wasn't here when I started
Will see the outline of Crazy Horse astride a mount,
And even if it takes a hundred years it might get done.
So, what about me? It's not for me,
Just ask who built the Sphinx or Europe's cathedrals?
All that matters is that it's there,
It's art—and I'm honored that these people,
Whose ancestors were here ten thousand years ago,
Asked me to make this. I have to keep faith with them.
This is art, and the frame is the sky and mountains,
And without this I am nothing,
So I'll go back to work now."

1977

KANSAS CITY STARS

Rolling through the corn-box counties, the slaughterhouse states.
Power line stanchions are robots in the fields.
Empty auto hauler looks like a mantis on wheels.
A sign in Illinois: *WILLIE & WAYLON*
                    AUG 28
You can't miss the message that repeats.
GAS FOOD PHONE LODGING. The Mutual Network.
Listening to Mighty Clouds of Joy on a Black blues station,
Russell and I cross the Mississippi outside St. Louis,
Cherry sun melting down.

Night infects Missouri. We decide to push for K.C.
Church radio beams through the grass-scented air—
Six pastors at once, one, a Red hater, offers the Christian Defense Packet
Stuffed with a Bible and a rifle. Thank God, "WLS, The Rock of Chicago,"
Breaks through the testaments, spinning "She loves you, yeah, yeah, yeah."
A dense auto-pack roars around banked curves
Like Al Junior and pals at the Pocono 500 earlier today.
Locked onto a nest of hits, we slice the night, burning standard gas.
Near the end of a marathon the brain flattens out, unable to transmit—
Motion is habit, the body moves by heart.
With four more states chalked up, we rest in the HoJo Lodge,
Sixth and Main, deep in a raw-beef city.
Kansas City Royals. Kansas City Chiefs.

The next night I sleep at the home of a woman I used to chase,
And wake on the edge of the Rockies.
She's with a welder and patchwork couples near the Air Force Academy.
Strange, yet so predictable to see her in this context—

The two of us like the rest of us, trying on the West for size.
After ten hours of Kansas farm houses anchored in swells of grain,
We had crossed into Kit Carson County under a blueberry ripple sky.
We praised sunflowers, took a whiff of sage.

In the morning, my compact crawls through Monarch Pass,
Swings north to Grand Junction, gliding through crusty geology:
Rocks shaped like body organs, ceaseless range, massive plateaus,
Vast arrangements of land and sky molded by wind tools,
Earth like Earth when only insects scraped the ground.
On Route 70 we notice the Ranch Exit signs,
But figure it's a trick to keep Russians away from our missiles.
Only the government, Secretary of De-Fence,
Would erect miles of such precise wire-and-post.
The red-and-sand terrain and distant layered expanse
On its way to ash, to dust, the western hide,
Cragville, the Plain of Mars, stone region.

We bolt south, climb into the Kaibab Forest,
Emerging amidst a scene of copper buttes
And the curled whip of a two-lane on the desert floor.
We zip past black-haired Navajo kids tending jewelry shacks.
At the Grand Canyon, fog and mist blow off to reveal the "boss ditch."
Near Ash Fork, Arizona, we pick up Route 66, arrow to Los Angeles.
A strange August rain drenches the Mojave.

Mississippi Delta Blues *Ballets Russes*

Muddy Waters (McKinley Morganfield) and George Balanchine (Giorgi Balanchivadze) both died on April 30, 1983.

America's all over the map.
Pick your plague, grab your cure.
There's no front curtain, no wall in back.
Every ticket has its price,
Any fence is full of holes,
And it's an open field from Montana to Canada.
America's all over the map.
It's a human soup boiled from scratch in gypsy pots,
Crazed vessels, rare skillets, iron bowls that were stashed in bags,
Lugged by hands of every language over purple hills,
Along the glacier trail, through a plasma sky, straight from the steppes.
America's all over the map, its mix a staple crop.
Muddy Waters pirouettes on steam-guitar, spreads the blues on canvas.
He's a rolling stone in the bayou, a boatman on the Volga.
There's a French Quarter balalaika, there's a jazz master in Red Square,
There's George Balanchine in a golden cowboy suit.

Don't Tell Jesse Helms

A hummingbird sucks red syrup from a tube at a brick bungalow
Where I'm hearing one of the region's foundation stories.
Mud-green ceramic catfish decorate an heirloom sideboard.
On the Salem side of a Carolina city branded by tobacco,
There's an old part settled by Moravians, neighbors of the Bohemians,
United Brethren who favored a ritual "lovefeast" of sweet buns and wine.
The German Protestants who walked south from Pennsylvania
Made a church community whose history museum today
Says those early Americans believed in radical sharing:
From each according to his ability, to each according to his needs.

Red Mud Road

Not brown-soil film but terra cotta dust, grainy on the porch table
Not far from where rebel fighters chewed their last dry corn.
Big lady waves at a rider coming her way, past the white church
And graveyard full of flags set against a heavy-set blue-green hill.
Jays yak in the branches. One pink geranium stuffs a pot,
And in my brother's side garden the mossy cement frog sits
Like a gone prince, disconsolate among brilliant marigolds.
Kudzu roots dredge so deep they tap wells in drought years.
Farmers say the nitro-weed's greedy tendrils will snare a calf.
There's tobacco to spare, chickens slowing down for autumn.
A hawk cleaves wind above pine homes near the highway,
The bird's shadow sailing in a fallow sea. A little okra, pinto beans,
Cherry tomatoes make a garden. The sun's saffron eye erupts.
Clouds are whiffs of smoke from mouths of just-blasted cannon.

Virginia Lines

To the tune of constant bird song
A money cat jumps in the sun.

Call and Response

So, a poet said a poet said,
"Now that Tennessee is dead,
We all have to go back home.
I'll pack my case and hickory comb,
Quit this shiny palm tree coast,
And re-set my foundation posts."

Meeting the Writers in Keysville

MY SISTER-IN-LAW DIANNE AND I drove south on Route 5 outside Farmville, Virginia, in the steamy heat of a mid-June suppertime. She had invited me to speak to her writing class at Southside Virginia Community College in Keysville close to North Carolina. The town's population was fewer than one thousand. The week before I had scanned her students' compositions responding to assignments such as "Definition and Classification," "Process Analysis," and "Personal Narratives." The twenty-five students, mostly men and women with full-time jobs, studied two nights a week in three-hour sessions for this five-week intensive course.

They wrote about "Pride" and "How to Hunt Squirrels." I learned that cucumber skins ward off cockroaches because the peelings affect roaches the way a skunk's odor repels a human. In the squirrel essay, the author explains that his wife refuses to cook "the rat" and he laments, "O, well, no squirrel with gravy and onions tonight!" One woman profiled her sister's boyfriend who crashed his girlfriend's car in "Nightmare on Escort Street."

Listening to golden oldies on the car radio, we passed ancient oaks whose full boughs register the slightest breeze. Here and there someone mowed a front lawn or walked slowly on the shady side. Modest town centers featured brand-name gas stations and mass-market product signs. The buildings repeated red brick and white trim.

Dianne asked me to read poems and talk about why I write. I thought the best I could offer the class would be a sense of what it is like to be a writer. Inside the one-level brick structure, the college corridors smelled of institutional floor wax and disinfectant, the aroma of American public buildings. Students were at their desks when we arrived, and after some housekeeping Dianne introduced me.

Recently, I had met Jo Carson from East Tennessee at a public-art conference in Durham, North Carolina. She wrote a book of vivid monologues and dialogues in the voices of her neighbors. Her work shows how a writer can conjure up a particular culture and place. Jo thinks of herself as an "eavesdropper" in Appalachia, who collects stories and composes poems and plays that contain strands of human truth. Here she is musing on the complications of neighborly behavior: "The man don't understand/he's doin a favor/when he takes and eats them damn zucchini,/and when he pays me for 'em,/when he pays me for 'em/ it's me ends up beholden to him." I read from the section about work in Carson's book *Stories I Ain't Told Nobody Yet*, and then shared my poems. For about an hour I spoke about landscape, history, and the origins of some of the poems I had read. At one point I asked if anyone could name a living American poet. No names were offered, so I wrote on the board: Alice Walker, Charles Wright, Lucille Clifton, Wendell Berry.

I also told the class about Tom O'Grady, a poet with a vineyard of French wine grapes who teaches with Dianne's husband, my brother David, at Hampden-Sydney College. In one of his books, *The Farmville Elegies*, O'Grady turns over the earth in a place now familiar to him, a relative newcomer who put down a stake: "I enter its echoes head down, wondering/who first loved on these floorboards/and who carried their solitude/up the stairs." (from "Living in Another Man's House"). From Jo Carson's region there is Jeff Daniel Marion, whose name made me stop on the contents page of a literary magazine when I saw it the first time. Another Marion with poems? We were catching up to the Lowells (James Russell, Amy, and Robert). I wanted to know him, so I ordered a book, *Out in the Country, Back Home*, and then (astonishingly) met him a year later when he read near my home at a private high school attended by a daughter of a friend of mine. Another writer who goes deep in the surrounding soil and society, Marion gets the picture and song just right: "Always there is a backporch/its screen door ajar/framing an old woman who is/pitching water outside,/the water arching its back/like the cat, ready to rub/her legs." ("Watercolor of an East Tennessee Farm"). These are poets to know in Keysville. Passing through Montana in the 1940s, Jack Kerouac wrote this in one of his journals: "In a drugstore window I saw a book on sale—so beautiful!—*Yellowstone Red*, a story of a man in the early days of the valley, & his tribulations & triumphs. Is this not better reading in Miles City than the *Iliad*?—their own epic?"

The students leaned in. Rather than keen attentiveness, it could have been that they were trying hard to understand me through my thick Boston accent. A group of uniformed nurses in the front desks responded at the right moments. Someone asked about writer's block. I said I worked on other forms of writing when the poetry dried up. I told one man that I shied away from love poems because of the masterful tradition of that type of poem in the English language, from Shakespeare on down. I had taken the advice that Rilke gives to the young poet in his letters. I said there are a hundred entry points when starting to write; each writer has to look for the daylight or starlight. Unlike at my guest appearance at my nephew's county high school the week before, nobody asked if I was a Republican.

As the end, four students asked me about publishing their work. One woman, upset that she left her poems at home, promised to mail them to me. She had written five. A man said he had a short story collection ready. I referred him to *Writer's Market* and the *Small Press Directory*. He wrote opinion essays for local newspapers and read all the new fiction he could find. Another woman copied my address into her notebook without saying why. Somebody asked if my books were in nearby bookstores.

Dianne was surprised. Maybe these aspirations are not something you tell the teacher. I told her I had seen the same thing happen a dozen times at readings I'd attended or at my own events. When I judged an annual poetry contest for a small city newspaper a few years before more than 1,000 poems were submitted by people in the paper's circulation area. Poetry is more like knitting than most people realize. It's out there on side-streets and mountaintops, in comfortable living rooms and rusted trailers up on cement blocks. New England poet Donald Hall said poetry is not dead even though some know-it-alls are trying to murder it. At readings there is always a person who slides up from the side to tell the guest writer that he or she, too, is a writer and to ask if it is okay to send a few pieces to get a response.

The writers in Keysville heard something new about American poetry. They will do their homework for two more weeks. Several of them will keep writing. Perhaps a few will pick up a shiny hardcover book of poems on the New Arrivals table in the public library or stop to read a poem in a magazine at the dentist's office. Maybe one of them will change some lives with words.

1989

two

Blood Alley, Fat City

Stockton's wide streets have no frost heaves,
Just dry heat and shade seekers,
Parakeets on orange crates,
And a rusty bus of tomato pickers—
Chicano field workers and dusty whites and blacks
Who'll strip cannery plants for a day's pay.

In the channel a freighter
Docks near checkered silos
Under the same daybreak haze
Muffling skid row, Tuxedo Lane,
And sprinkled lawns on El Dorado.

Palms garnish the front of St. Mary's
Where Spanish guitars and tambourines
Play the four o'clock Mass;
Next door in a parish gym
Gloves slap bags, rope ticks a gritty floor.

In suburban kitchens and dens
Beautiful Californians,
Up from dinner tables and television,
Open windows on Robin Hood Drive
To hear pool filters hum
And watch Mt. Diablo absorb the red sun.

SUNDAY MORNING IN CANADA

The odd offering of Canadian news
Sprayed from a San Diego tower
To my radio an hour north by car
Raised questions about fact and happening.
Parliamentary debates affect Yellowknife
And St. Jean de Matha. Beirut smoke and
Olympic medals garnish breakfast plates
In Toronto. And here I am in salsa country,
Eavesdropping on continental bulletins,
Acting as if it must matter to know as much
As I can about anything being done anywhere.
I can't stop listening to the planet getting older.
Somehow I'll need this as much as the fruit
And vegetables at Ralph's Market. Why else
Would I be able to tap into the line?
Still, there's probably a better reason
I keep turning north when I'm so far south
That people walk here from Mexico.
Reports flow back and forth like
Weather ridges, high pressure systems,
Like acid rain and waterfowl. All in the air.

DANA POINT

On Seville the condo units cozy up like pleasure boats in their slips.
Across the street, garage industry, two women sew custom-made bikinis.
A chocolate parcel truck picks up special orders every afternoon.
Richard Dana quit Harvard College, set off to cure his eyesight.
His ship Pilgrim rounded the Cape—rain-wind, salt-snow, fried air.
This Pacific strip, Capistrano's beachhead, hails the writer in bronze.
In Vons' Market on Ortega Drive, handling a blue plastic bowl
Molded in a plant upriver from the Lowell textile mills,
I recalled the ship's cargo, stuff we swap, like that tough New England
Cloth. Christmas 1834. Just north of the equator. Dana writes,
"It brought us no holiday." Twenty days from California,
A hundred-plus from Boston, provisions ran out.
Jump to 1983. Pilgrim II rigged with colored lights and streamers.
Flashbulbs pop in Dana West Marina at the Yuletide parade of boats—
All the kids and captains harmonize on "Little Saint Nick."

SAN CLEMENTE

We asked if the system had worked when it was through.
The drumming of *Post* reporters in '72
Had White House bag-men scrambling in the stew.
Instead of counting dead Viet Cong, they dreamt payoff sagas,
Talking "stonewall" and "tossing out the big enchilada."
Credible Dean blew a factual whistle for Sam Ervin.
Milhous squirmed, but knew Spiro had slipped the pen.
The Saturday Night Massacre of Cox drew mail by tons.

Oval Office lawyers and priests trotted out candid lines.
Dick TV'd his edited transcripts, said he wasn't lying.
But Judge Sirica persisted, the full Supreme
Court said, "Give," and Rodino, red-eared from screen-
Ing tapes, found the high crime. Impeachment's Goliath sword
Sent Nixon scuttering west in a dethroned whirlybird.

CAPISTRANO VALLEY

A run of deep pink
like winter lava
along the freeway,
and on the far ridge
a twin color splash
below house frames,
raw boards in full sun.
Gliding north,
savoring orange blossoms,
I catch the white buildings,
terra cotta roofs,
and dull shark's teeth
of Santa Ana Mountains
biting the sky.

THE BLACKFEET INDIAN PENCIL

I've been told I'm part Indian, but don't believe it.
North American tribe. Canadian blood.
Snow country natives. First people to make love on the continent.
The Marion, Ohio, All-Indian NFL Team of 1922
Fielded Arrowhead, Black Bear, Deerslayer, Wrinkle Meat,
Laughing Gas, Red Fang, Baptiste Thunder, Lone Wolf, and Deadeye.
Indians made this pencil I'm using,
Same business as Henry Thoreau before his trip up the Merrimack River.
Like Jefferson and Lincoln, Marion spreads across the states,
Praise for the Swamp Fox, General Francis Marion,
Who tied the British in revolutionary knots down Carolina way.
Southerners captured the North's *Merrimack*, re-named the ship *Virginia*,
Then armored it for a clash with the Union's ironclad.
Marion Drive crosses Sunset Boulevard.
When actress Ruth Marion died in Carmel last week,
The L.A. *Times* praised her as "a stroke of good luck to her friends."
Her screen-star father had romanced Greta Garbo.
Jazz Age-script whiz Frances Marion earned Academy Awards.
I had not heard of the Hollywood Marions.
Costa Mesa, California, has a Merrimac Street.
In Missouri, one river is called Meramec.
The word can mean "Strong Place" in Algonkian,
Language of tribes from Massachusetts to the Rockies:
Pawtucket, Pemigewasset, Ojibwa, Cree, Fox
Shawnee, Arapahoe, Wamesit, and Blackfoot.

Helicopters for Turner Square

Iron chops the sky up and down this coast, from Camp Pendleton to the Marine air base at El Toro. Maybe it's the palm trees or because I'm picturing the surf sliding into Vietnam on the other hem of this ocean, but I can't help thinking these helicopters are from the war, the ones that carried wounded kids out of fire zones long enough ago that movies of the war seem old. I didn't have to go, but can't get rid of it. My draft number was 62 the year the call-ups were suspended, and I still don't know what I would have done. I keep reading Casey's *Obscenities* and Herr's *Dispatches*, drawn to the mayhem. I wonder if young Daniel Turner from my home back east was stationed in California before shipping out. Six years older than me, he was a sergeant in the Air Force when he died in Gia Dinh Province in 1969, a "ground casualty," per military records. A quiet guy who lived up the hill from my house, his name now tops a steel post set in a grassy crossroads where I caught my high school bus. Now it's a hero square: Turner Square. When I visited the bright black Wall in hot and steamy white-stone Washington, D.C., and felt the incisions in its mirror-face, I searched for Sergeant Turner's name among the names that hold up all the signs at all the intersections. His dates are 31 Jan 48, 17 Aug 69. Daniel R. Turner. He's on Panel 19 West, Row 57. Just like the neighborhood sign.

GOODBYE, LAGUNA

At the four-way stop on Glenneyre,
A Mercedes, a Jag, and a yellow Rolls
Stare at my basic green Lynx.
The ease of wealth deceives in Laguna Beach,
Lets me think luxury is not extraordinary.
A miniature composes in my side mirror:
Bleached surf-kids wait to cross Coast Highway,
Their swimsuits bright as crayons.
He's outside my picture, but I'm sure
The Greeter is hailing traffic this morning,
Long beard and staff his trademarks.
Across from the Art Market,
Gray Panthers are in position,
Holding placards that shout:
"No More Hiroshimas!" "Honk for Peace!"—
And the incredible athletic specimens
Gathered on beachside courts
Are loosening up for a little hoop.
And the women wear next to nothing.
Sun turns the whole place into dessert,
Vitamin-rich, sweet, but low-cal SoCal,
Absorbed by simply being here. Here,
Work seems unrelated to sweat.
Shop clerks and gallery keepers act as if
They're inside for diversion.
The Hotel Laguna valet kicks back in a lawn chair.
My Catholic-Liberal-Yankee conscience
Tells me someone must be suffering for this,
Somewhere there will be pain to pay,
But as far as I can see we're all smiling.

three

Marlborough Woods

Brown in their winter skins,
They rise up, lean pointers,
Borders of the wilderness.
Glass branches dip and sway,
And in the chilly distance
Across the top of Mount Monadnock,
Under a white flannel sun,
Wind blows the snow like cold smoke.

THE FROST FARM IN DERRY

I'm considering what to consider,
Looking for a clue
In this land and weather,
Same as the time he tramped through,
Catching burrs on trouser legs.
Leaves were just as red.
The same sun keeps winter off these stones
And trees of boiled bones.

THE BREAD AND PUPPET CIRCUS

Noon.
Bicentennial Circus pokes fun.
Pirate horsemen dance for squares. Witches curse war machines.
Peace plays in the barn. Satire in the meadow.
Uncle Sam as businessman. Father George in midget gear.
Power is slain while the weird horns parade.
Full of free sourdough rye, celebrants watch angels.
Angels of ecology, angels of trees, angels of Temptation.
Dreamscapes of Swan Lakes. Folksingers from Chile.
Biblical charades. Kids' cardboard games.
Women gypsies, loose and long-haired, leap over bales.
A man with gold curls tucked up in a tan burnoose.
Children draped in yellow linen and red sashes.
Denim ramblers eating vegetable sandwiches.
Fiddlers in frock coats and cowboy hats.
Rural neighbors showing what they know.
Craftsmen downing cider. Grandmothers playing guitars.
Professors under monk-hooded ponchos.

Toward evening.
Cannon and lanterns and stars and banners in the arena.
Suppertime hush in the white pine woods.
Mute priests and man-ponies act out Bach spirit music.
The silence of chanters padding on rusty duff,
Their small bells the only sound.
A holy mask goes over Glover.
Vermont's green breath sings like a wheel.
Umbrellas mushroom on the grassy slope.
A Domestic Resurrection Pageant renews the Light.
Dragon-sized sheet-worm enters from the east.

Symbol theatre under the Crystalline Sphere.
A procession of red tongues snakes toward the drumbeats.
Shrieks of Aztec birds hawking in over the rise,
Wide rigid wings slicing hard rain.
Chains of fire, a stream of torches,
Amid wild pipe and hubcap and brass cymbal
And hunk metal clanking signal music.
Birds and Fire renew the Light.
A shaman on stilts dripping with gold spangles
Thumps the Earth like a drum.

GLAZIERS

On the route to Calais
We go over the whale's back,
A stretch like roller coaster track
Where the land drops down
On both sides for 300 feet.
Thick brush hides how steep.
Later, smoking across coastal flats,
We see a machine that pounds sand.
The glass on our truck is rattling in the slats.

Winterport

Bowls of blue plums in the snow.
A potato freighter plows through frosty aqua.
Lobster boats are fierce with icicles.
Heavy caskets of winter pile up.
The furnace roars, eating apple wood.
Jackets and boots are by the door,
Canning jars crowd the cellar,
And everywhere the gulls holler.

MAINE HERON

A blue heron waits an hour,
Shows patient power
In a one-man soup line,
Disregards time
In favor of a single mind—
The key to catching fish.
The heron squawks,
Shoves off with awkward grace,
Gawking into flight,
Pole legs folding,
Kite wings holding,
Then uncranking
Like awnings,
Whacking light wind
Past feathers like
Blue-gray saw-toothed fringe.
The heron stands like a sinister old goat,
A crook in an overcoat—
Chin tucked in,
Legs stem-thin,
Skinny neck, collar up close
To a frown and long nose—
Stuck in the mud in a standing doze.

Rat Race

We hadn't spoken for ages before the phone rang.
I knew it was him when he ordered 25 double-cheese pizzas to go.
"What the hell you doing up there?" I yelled, knowing why he'd called.
My new book was the crowbar that pried him out of the woodwork.
We jumped into our old fooling. He told me about his year-old son
And that his accountant had just confirmed a big profit year.
His house, the Otis Palace, gets NBA games via satellite.
"So, what's new with you?" he yelled back. I filled him in a bit.
He can't imagine leaving Maine. "I'm okay. The world's crazy.
The Swiss just killed the Rhine River. Saw it on TV. Chemicals.
I should've gone more north, maybe the sticks of Canada,
But I'm still way ahead of schedule for retirement."
"I don't own a house yet," I said, "not married. You're fine.
See you in April when the rivers get fat on snowmelt."

BURYING ISLAND

Marking tide levels, Steve bucks home routines.
Above the rockweed cove he built a cabin,
An all-weather den ferried piecemeal in his dory
And hauled up a cliff on his back. Spruce root sideways.
In the rocky soil, trees are straw to nor'easters.
He picks up splintered sea-snails gulls drop onto rocks.
Clam chips speckle a sandbank where the Mound People ate fish.
Sand fleas jitter the seaweed beach at noon.
Cormorants clatter into flight, wings slapping madly off water.
Bright eelgrass oscillates at high tide. Moss pads a rough ledge
Where a head with quartz eyes stares like an Easter Island giant.
At night, the Bar Harbor Hills, a hump serpent on the coast,
Show a necklace of traffic, part of the turnpike herd,
Sill roaring out of the toll booths like thoroughbreds.

Ball of Confusion, Sea of Tranquility

1.

There's a sign at the Bangor Shopping Mall seeking the owner of an inflatable woman found in the parking lot. Did she fly off the roof of her apartment house? Did she escape from a car when the owner went shopping? Did she step on a nail while running away?

2.

In one dream, I'm piloting an oil tanker in a small harbor. The ship keeps scraping the bottom and bashing the dock. The engine speeds up without warning. I keep forgetting my hands are on the wheel.

3.

John Haines quotes Edwin Muir in *Living Off the Country*: "Our minds are possessed of three mysteries: where we came from, where we are going, and since we are not alone, but members of a countless family, how we should live with one another."

4.

Marie and I couldn't get enough of each other that summer at the Ellsworth Rotary Club's Annual Blueberry Pancake Breakfast and Winter Harbor Lobster Festival. There were so many johnnycakes to flip, so many hot potatoes to toss, so many shells to crack.

5.

I saw the aurora borealis beyond the Chair and Swan outlined in starry dots. The moon surfaced like a yellow stone, then turned the color of peace. Ghost fish leapt at light like the first lizards plucking feet from the muck, dazzled eyes turned up.

CROSSING THE LINE

So long, Pembroke and Meddybemps.
Hello, Andalusia and Machu Picchu.
No more Coast Guard theologians.
No more Jonesboro jazz trawlers.
No Eastport sardine sandwiches.
No black flies in the birch-bark canoe.
Deliver me from ancient holy motors.
Get me topographical love.
Get me to the liberty grange.
Get me to the fluent news.

TRASH PICKERS BY THE CAPE HIGHWAY

Triumphant music pouring forth
As my car glides over the Sagamore Bridge.
Scrub pine off the highway.
The trash pickers of Scusset
Have pilgrim sand in their cuffs.
Orange safety belts across their backs.
Yellow plastic bags of junk.
The gray Cape. A wide wale sky.
I want to see the result of my work.
I want to do a simple job and like it.

The Yellow Gate

We crossed Harvard Square at twilight.
Bluegrass troubadours caught coins in an alley.
Our lemonade at the Café Algiers was tall and sour.
We kept our voices down. At slim tables
Night's royalty sipped pomegranate soda.
New Yorker couples puffed twin thin cigars.
A temptress who could have ruled a sandy country
Ordered a cup of goat yogurt, and next door
Jugglers tossed fire outside the place with the yellow gate:
Women upstairs would peal sheer grace if they were bells.
A man stretches muscle strings into a physical region
Where the dance will decide what the body can do.
In this great well of action, rhythm bounds out of beings
As if they were trees releasing their inner rings.

Joseph Among the Shawabtis

My small blond boy standing like a guard studies alabaster dolls that were carried to Boston long ago, spoils of the museum's Nubian digs. He's looking back through artifacts to an Egypt in translation, our version full of holes and interpretive moments. His mother and I return by habit to the cool stones and hammered gold. The Rulers of Kush laid up a thousand non-action figures in the tomb of King Taharka for an Underworld work gang. Invested with its power to calm, Joe's soft yellow duck would fit in among the mute servants. I hope the story boggles his future mind the way it stumps me, using my head to piece together fragments, notes, material culture out of context. Joseph stares at the Shawabtis like one of the Spielberg movie kids, the one who meets spindly aliens floating down their spaceship ramp. Joe may live to learn who really drew the diagram for Thebes and taught the Pharaohs picture-writing.

SHARKS RIP THE NETS

Sharks rip the nets,
Keeping us from taking too much.
Silver fish dive. Engines run hot.
Cottage glass shines like blue gin.
Sand wheat inscribes the dunes.
Planks and long country poles
Lean against houses until patching days.
Oil thickens in a can.
Drawers of yarn will empty after Christmas,
The artery a sheet-metal freeze.
Fear of surf that could blast a body to cream
Puts a leash on the scout.
For the sight of a lilac blooming,
I'd like to sue the stars.

French King Bridge

Eight of us gave ourselves an assignment:
Climb a hundred feet up a rocky slope, from the Connecticut River
To the deck of French King Bridge, a beauty-contest winner.
And the bridge was as gorgeous as a battleship—
Black trusses whose rivets popped in sunny highlight,
Beaming metal tinted by a powder-blue November sky.
The structure shone a midnight blue, like a black-and-blue,
Like a bruise, almost like a plum, in the blue-sky morning.
We skidded on gravel, picking a route between gully and soft spots,
Bracing against the abutment, glancing back just once to scare ourselves
On the way to the odd gift we'd give ourselves:
A sense of self as tiny as a figure in a Chinese landscape scroll,
On top of a prize view of Pioneer Valley
Slightly past the wild color peak.

Merrimacport

Driving north through the summer-green valley, I tick off place names: Andover, Lawrence, Haverhill, and then Merrimacport. Next time I'll exit right to see past the sign. It must be less than small-city Newburyport, where money-running merchants made the killing that raised the mills upriver, toward the interior, where falls foam in the rush—clear power rounding bedrock jags. There were once ship-masters and boat-builders in the yards from Cape Ann to Portsmouth; captains on High Street; hands who turned their backs on the square clocks and tower bells and red stacks of mill towns; traders, counters, and sail-makers; lumbermen felling pines; mast-makers and carpenters hammering ships' knees; coopers, wheelwrights, and smiths; food-handlers and butchers; painters, spice-grinders; tailors and seamstresses; hatters and pipe-makers; cobblers, corn-farmers, orchard-men; the physician and ministers; teachers, midwives, selectmen, and stable hand; map-maker and depth-sounder; the lookout, the scout, the soldier; spirit-maker, tavern maid, and dry-goods seller; boarding house-keeper and sheriff. All these types pacing a day, in sight of a sea-stuck forest past the dock, the working boats and broad ships just back or ready to go. What cargo Merrimacport? What story in the hold? What distance Merrimacport, where the river runs to salt? The river runs past Deer and Ram islands, past Seal and Woodbridge islands, past Gangway Rocks, Half Tide Rocks, and Toothpick, past Black Rocks and Black Rock Creek and Outer Badger, past Plum Island and Plum Island River, past Pine Island River, Joppa Flats, and Salisbury Beach. And all that the ocean brought—knowledge, material, gold—came landward down the plank, stamped the ground, made the next thing happen. The sea took a bite of sand. Moon in the glass—wave cream, rapid's mane—pepper in a jar on the shelf—sailcloth needles, square nails, boots with a belt to match. The lighthouse keeper made a hole in the fog.

THE WAR PLACE (10.)
GULF WAR NOTEBOOK (JANUARY-MARCH 1991), AN EXCERPT

Feb. 15. Iraq's Revolutionary Command Council says Iraq is prepared to withdraw from Kuwait in compliance with United Nations Security Council Resolution 660. The offer is linked to an overall Middle East conflict settlement, including the Palestinian issue. U.S. officials are skeptical about this announcement. Military operations continue. The Coalition leaders (U.S., France, Great Britain, and Saudi Arabia) reject the proposal.

On his way to his vacation home in Kennebunkport, Maine, President George H. W. Bush stops in Andover, Massachusetts, to visit the Raytheon Company plant that manufactures the Patriot missile, "the Scud-buster." Each missile costs $1.1 million. I'm listening live on National Public Radio as the crowd chants, "USA! USA! USA!" With the President are Mrs. Bush and Massachusetts Governor William Weld. George Bush attended Phillips Academy in Andover; he was born in this state. The announcer says, "Welcome to Raytheon in Andover, Massachusetts. This is the home of the Patriot Missile." And then the national anthem plays. The President at this moment is about 15 minutes away from me by car—about twelve miles up Route 133. A minister from Harvard University offers an invocation. "Let us pray. Keep us mindful of those who are facing danger for our sake." Another speaker says it fills him with pride to see the missile perform magnificently in the service of our country. He calls it the best equipment that American technology can produce.

Tom Phillips, Chairman of Raytheon, says, "Ladies and gentlemen, the President of the United States," and the President begins speaking: "I view it as an honor to be here, the home of the men and women who build the Scud-busters. Earlier today our hopes were lifted, and I expressed regret that the Iraqi statement was a cruel hoax. Iraq must withdraw without conditions, and there will be no linkage to other problems in the area. (applause) The legitimate government must be returned to Kuwait. The Coalition will continue its efforts to force compliance with the U.N. resolutions, every one of them. (applause) The Iraqi people can take matters into their own hands and force Saddam Hussein to stop, and then comply with the resolutions. We have no argument with the people of Iraq. Our differences are with that brutal dictator in Baghdad. I'm going to stay with it. We are going to prevail, and our soldiers are going to come home with their heads high."

The President refers to the split-second accuracy of the Patriot missile-defense system. Since mid-August, Raytheon has been running three shifts a day, seven days a week, building Patriots in Andover. "The Patriot works because of patriots like you," says the President, "and I came to say thanks to each and every one of you." This is a triumph of American technology, he continues, that is pushing forward the bounds of progress critical to our competitiveness. He praises the men and women who operate the system in the field. Describing the Patriot, experts say it is like shooting a bullet with a bullet, a revolution in air defense. Critics said the system was plagued with problems, but they have been shown to be wrong. The Patriot is 41 for 42—of the 42 Scuds engaged, 41 have been intercepted. George Bush says the word "Scud" like he's spitting out bad food. He says, "Missile defense threatens no one. We know this is a dangerous world. All it takes is one renegade regime to target innocent civilians." He says he is less impressed by theories than he is by nations with the strength and will to defend themselves.

"Thank God for the Patriot missile. Operation Desert Storm is on course and on schedule. We will control the timing of this engagement, not Saddam Hussein. Make no mistake about it, Kuwait will be liberated. A tyrant's attempt to rain terror from the sky has been blunted. President Woodrow Wilson said, 'In war there are a thousand forms of duty.'

May God bless our troops and their families and the United States of America!" (cheers, applause, cheers, shouting).

Feb. 16. Day 31 of the Gulf War. "We continue to strike and re-strike strategic targets," says the day's briefer. There were 700 sorties in KTO (Kuwaiti Theater of Operations) today. "We continue to interdict lines of communication and supply." As of today, 29 Coalition aircraft have been lost in combat (20 U.S. and nine allied). On the Iraqi side, 42 aircraft have been lost in combat, 36 fixed-wing and six helicopters. So far, 65 Scuds have been launched.

Feb. 18. Iraq is considering a new plan offered by the U.S.S.R. The Coalition continues to prosecute the war. The first mine damage to Coalition ships has been reported: two U.S. ships damaged. In England, two bombs exploded, killing one person and injuring 40 others. The IRA is suspected of being responsible. In Amherst, Massachusetts, a young man burned himself to death in a war protest. He doused himself with paint thinner and set himself on fire. He left a peace sign next to his body. This reminds me of the self-immolations during the Vietnam War. The man who set himself on fire was the son of two *Boston Globe* reporters.

Feb. 20. Peace negotiations intensify. The U.S.S.R. is pressing its plan. An Iraqi official flew to China. Iran says Iraq is ready to withdraw from Kuwait unconditionally. The Allies keep attacking. President Bush says he is grateful for the U.S.S.R.'s attempts, but feels the plan is still not acceptable. There have been ground engagements along the Saudi-Kuwait border. Iraqi forces were heavily damaged. The U.S. casualties: 1 KIA (Killed in Action), seven wounded. In one attack on a bunker complex by U.S. helicopter and security forces, 400 EPWs (Enemy Prisoners of War) were taken.

Feb. 22. President Bush gives Iraq until tomorrow noon EST to withdraw from Kuwait or a ground offensive will begin. Bush says Iraq has started a scorched-earth policy in Kuwait with some 160 of 900 oil wells set on fire. He says the U.S.S.R. proposal is not acceptable to the Allied Coalition.

Feb. 23. 11.45 a.m. Peter Arnett of CNN reports live from Baghdad. A night-lens green sky over Baghdad is lit with anti-aircraft fire. One minute to 12 o'clock noon—CNN broadcasts commercials on teacher recruitment, car sales, a tool supply company, and an investment firm.

Noon. Live from the United Nations in New York City, there is a report that the Iraqi foreign minister has responded positively to the Coalition "statement." Live from Tel Aviv, Israel, CNN broadcasts a scene with air raid signals sounding an alarm for a Scud missile attack. The U.N. Security Council is in session. The United States Ambassador to the U.N., Thomas Pickering, wants Iraq to clarify its response to the ultimatum. Live TV from Baghdad shows bombs exploding. Live from the White House, the word is that there is nothing to report as the deadline passed. "We are monitoring the situation." The President and Secretary of State are at Camp David. At noon, there is a huge explosion near the Baghdad hotel where the CNN crew is based—probably a cruise missile. Kuwaiti resistance fighters report that Iraqi soldiers are killing Kuwaiti civilians. They report "atrocities."

Peter Jennings of ABC-TV says "We don't know if the 'mother of all battles' is about to begin, but Saddam Hussein now finds himself in the mother of all corners." The U.S.S.R.'s Foreign Minister says the Iraqi minister agreed to some of the conditions in President Bush's ultimatum. Everyone is waiting for an authoritative statement about this from the U.N. The Pentagon reports that Coalition forces are jamming Iraqi military radio frequencies—usually a prelude to an invasion.

10 p.m. EST. President Bush announces that he has authorized General Norman Schwarzkopf to use all force necessary to eject Iraqi forces from Kuwait. CBS News reports that Coalition forces are six to eight miles inside Kuwait. In Israel, violinist Isaac Stern played to an audience wearing gas masks after an air raid siren sounded. The orchestra left the stage, but Stern played on alone. All history is biography, someone wrote. "This will not stand," Bush warned last August.

four

Climbing the Tenement Stairs

AS A KID, I HEARD THE RELATIVES on both sides chatting in cut-and-spliced Canadian American-Franglais French, their tongues waggling strings of words so fast I caught each third phrase, and then patched in conversational sense. They sat at the maple table drinking coffee, whiskey, tea, beer, tonic—rattling on about Little Canada, the packed tenement life between the canal and the river, and the Centralville of St. Louis de France parish, just this side of the Dracut frontier woods. When my French Canadian-American mother was a girl in Centralville she would not cross the Aiken Street Bridge to the enclave she considered low-class French, but still wound up with my father, a Cheever Street product.

I heard stories about Français of the Honey Wagon making rounds to collect pig-swill. During the '36 Flood, he herded his swine onto the porch, then up to the first, second, and, finally, third floor as water crested halfway up the block in Rosemont Terrace. And there was the time my grandfather's store burned. Waiting for friends one night, he lit the oil stove. He and his chums drank a good time before heading home across the river's ice. As soon as he sat down, a neighbor rushed in with the news.

On Saturday, a boy would pick up bean pots and deliver them to the bakery where they were retrieved the next morning for a big bean breakfast before or after Mass, depending on the family's level of devotion. Kids walked the canals during drain-downs, scouring muddy beds for treasure. The same kids stole cloth from the ragman's wagon when he stepped inside to do business. They sold his stuff back to him on the next corner. The kids scooped fresh-water shrimp from the Merrimack and boiled them with potatoes on the river rocks for a feed. These French Canadian-American folks had marathon card games, moving from house to house. New Year's Day meant pork pie, noise, and sweets.

When she was young my mother was scalded in a cooking accident.

My father climbed a set of tenement stairs in *Petit Canada* to see a man known to have healing power, a medicine man, seventh son of a seventh son. She recovered and testified to this.

The North American carpenter Joseph Marion came to the States in 1881. His son Doda, born in Quebec, married in Lowell and died here in 1946. His grandson Wilfrid, the one with the store, is alive in his 90s. His great grandson Marcel, my father, a man with a trade, was born and died in Lowell. In his 40s, he often spent half the year in central California working for a wool growers' co-op because the money was so good. He'd tour sprawling sheep ranches up and down the San Joaquin Valley, speaking French to the Basque ranchers.

My two brothers, an artist and a scholar, married teachers. Their kids expect a college education. Doda's wife, Rosalba, operated looms in Lowell a hundred years ago. For the moment, our Marions can't reach back farther than merchant Nicholas marrying Marie Guéric in Normandy in 1665. He died in the New Old World of Quebec.

My mother, Doris, sold coats and dresses in a women's clothing store downtown for 30 years. When I was small, my father, brothers, and I drove her to South Station in Boston, where she boarded a silver rail car bound for a retail training program at Charles of the Ritz in New York City. We thought it was her big career break, but she came home early with the flu. She never complained about that and won praise for her work in her career. I found the training manual years later while cleaning out her bedroom bureau.

We've traced her side, Roy and LeRoy, to 1638 in Normandy, where Louis LeRoy married Anne LeMâitre in St. Remi de Dieppe. Her line comes through Nicholas and Jeanne, Nicholas II and Madeleine, Étienne and Marie, Pierre and Hélène, Antoine and Angelique, René and Marie, Damase and Marie, Philippe and Antoinette, and Joseph and Cécile Berubé Roy, wed in St. Jean-Baptiste Church in 1916, down to my mother, who died this year. The two lines converge at the river bend. All the pieces aren't in place—all the poor scramblers who lived, worked, loved, suffered, laughed, and died. I'm naming the names as I go.

1989

THE WAR PLACE (10.)
WORLD WAR II

PART ONE

1944.

From the Pacific came a report about my mother's brother Charles: "At the base of Mount Auger on Guam, the 21-year-old Marine corporal had moved to outflank Japanese machine-gunners who had pinned down his entire company. His squad scrambled over volcanic rock and tropical stubble on the back slope. Men cut by saber-grass knew not to cry out. After climbing for four hours, Charles and his men came up behind the enemy trenches. The Marine riflemen drove the defenders into the open, but two counter-flanking Japanese nearly surprised the Americans. Corporal Roy said, 'The motion the grenade-thrower had to make to knock his grenade against his helmet to set off the charge—that was what saved me. I had enough rifle training to be able to unlock my rifle in that instant to get it up and fire four rounds. I got both of them.'" With the fight boiling, my uncle dug a foxhole on the spot and spent the night near a dead Japanese soldier. Making his way back to a rest station two days later, he was wounded by an artillery shell. He and 600 hurt Marines received their Purple Heart medals in a military-hospital ceremony attended by seven generals and seven admirals.

PART TWO

Pulling on their Civil Defense armbands, my parents, Doris and Marcel, climbed the tower stairs of the Old Yellow Meetinghouse in their New England town to watch for Nazi planes coming down the river path in the weeks after Japanese pilots attacked Pearl Harbor in Hawaii. That was two years before my father was drafted into the Army. He had a job in the essential wool industry, but by late 1944 all available men were being sent to fight.

"Somewhere in Germany, March 10, 1945

Sweetheart, Darling, I'm now somewhere in Germany, and I'm fine and well dear. Don't you worry sweet because I'm somewhere in Germany. Honey, believe me, I'll take very good care of myself dear. I've been assigned to the Third Army. I'm still with some of the boys I know, but I've lost contact with Vic. He must be assigned to the Third Army, too. Now you can send me a box, dear, candy bars, fudge, tissues, a box of good Fanny Farmer's candy. Don't send any cigarettes or blades or gum, I've got plenty of that. Honey, I love you with all my heart and the baby, too. I miss the both of you an awful lot, too. This will end soon, and I'll be coming home for good honey. Darling don't worry about me, I might not be able to write every day from now on, but whenever I'm able to I will dear, you can depend on that sweet. Give my address to everybody and give them my regards. All my love to you and Richard, and loads of kisses to honey. Good night and pleasant dreams honey. I love you terribly dear.

Love and kisses, yours lovingly, Marcel"

PATTERNS OF A PRAYER TOWN

Our Lady of the Bathtub shines white.
A flagpole becomes a stack of gold eggs.
Small dogwood tree vanishes; in its place a floating rosary.
There's a chain-link gate festooned with gaudy bulbs,
Shrubs lassoed blue, dormers outlined in radiant jelly beans—
Every other house decorated like a birthday cake.
City folk do it for you and me, for their kids and kids of passing strangers.
But what do the Martians think,
Gazing at us through super-powered telescopes?
What do they make of this season,
When it looks like a carnival has spread like flu through the neighborhoods?

PINKY'S GOSPEL

"That ashtray's so big you can do laundry in it! What are you up to now? Still reading those deep books? Make a communist out of yourself yet. In this country, all they're doing is building a big bureaucracy. Liberals are ruining the country. People don't give a goddamn—they say, 'Leave me alone. No matter what those guys are doing up there, what the hell, there's nothing I can do.' They're fed up. You can smell something going on. When it happens, it'll happen so fast it'll blow up. Everything is bad, nothing is good, it stinks. People who're one step ahead buy land and put a trailer on it. Taxes are ridiculous. Lawyers are running us. Lawyers are wrecking the country. It's unreal.

"And you, my sister, you need help. I don't know if anyone can help you. And your husband there, he's a jewel in the rough. What are you gonna do with an old horse like that—leave him in the stable, put a blanket on him?

"Have you heard from that homely girl I used to see, the other one there? She married the guy she was running with? Jesus! Hey, remember Ma and her beans? Ma would bake beans, and the old man would give her a pigeon, a pigeon in the pot—best damn thing I ever ate. I make beans, good beans, with molasses and bacon fat. Hey, I gotta go. Thank you, yup, bye now."

1976

STEEL RAIN

On a long street
By the black canal
There's a man alone
At the railing, counting
The leaves in the flow,
Watching a slice of moon
Above housing blocks
Drenched by a shower,
The roofs all washed and
Soaked by the steel rain.

DYLAN SINGS TO KEROUAC

The railroad earth,
The hot autumn earth,
The cemetery earth,
The Lincoln earth,
The November earth.

The dharma karma earth,
The Indian summer earth,
The Rolling Thunder earth,
The musical earth,
The deep dug earth.

The Lowell earth,
The afternoon earth,
The literary earth,
The cowboy poet earth,
The Minnesota earth.

The French-Canadian earth,
The old Jewish earth,
The Bicentennial earth,
The folk ground,
The quiet ground.

The round red earth,
The hay-colored earth,
The sunny leaves on earth,
The brown and red-brick leaves,
The yellow-orange leaves,
The golden red grave leaves.

1975

THE SANDBANK ON RIVERSIDE

For François Pelletier and his fellow voyageurs

There were so many universes in the grains of sand sliding off the cliff behind the plain concrete apartment strip on Riverside Street that we had to scoop up handfuls of the tan stuff, like golden nuggets panned out of Sutter's Creek in northern California in 1849, a place Merrimack River Valley wild men had raced toward in the Gold Rush, cutting trails to the West and getting themselves out to the new territories like the old French fur-hat voyagers in their papery canoes and wooden dugouts named Adventure and Money and LeRoy and Monseigneur, paddling through the unbelievably dark forests and the game-filled meadows of unfenced America, and the beds of those streams and creeks and rivers on which the canoes rode were cool sand like the sand we scooped into our pockets and torn envelopes and empty cigarette packs, treasure to be carried back to the homeland from this site of pilgrims, magic dust to be handed around for home altars, holy sand like holy water, holy for its ancient origin in the melting ice sheet that had plowed southward from the tip-top of the Earth, encasing North Pole, Yukon, Montreal, Franconia Notch, Mount Monadnock, Pawtucket Falls, Rosemont Basin, Beaver Brook, Pine Brook, and Riverside Street, where we got on our knees to collect this evidence of time and life and nature and force and flow and simple matter, here where the water once ran, where it sifted soil till it was as smooth as a beach, here where the glacier pressed its case until Mother Nature warmed up and hiked her frozen skirt high enough to show leg way north of Quebec City, here where Champlain might have turned the corner on his way inland from Newburyport on the Atlantic, after nosing into the river called Strong Place by the natives, here where descendants of continental migrants from Rivière du Loup and St. Jean de Matha settled on the banks of a river whose power drove wheels of industry and stoked imaginations of mill-makers and cathedral-builders, here where a young person in a room at night overlooking the sandbank could dream of writing and telling stories of all America, all the world, and all the cosmos, all the universes compressed into sand grains, each an infinitesimal model of all that's in and out and around, all we taste on our tongues like the salty seaweed in the soup from which we emerged.

2005

Majestik Linen

In a subterranean room roaring like a jet,
Sunday workers feed or unload machines,
Busy in twos and threes at their stations.
Plain as old-time mill operatives, they handle cloth by the mile:
Nursing-home pillow cases, dinner napkins, green scrubs from the ER,
Loved sheets, double-bleached butchers' aprons, hotel towels,
Well-fed tablecloths from a club luncheon.
The linen workers take it in and pass it on—their canvases unsigned.
A young woman catches my face in the window.
Instead of giving her a wave, any kind of nod,
I freeze like a common eavesdropper.
She turns back to her work, what most of us won't see
Unless we're in the Flats at the hour of the early Mass,
Following the drone of automatic washers
To a sunrise service recognized worldwide.
Their names are in the phone book with ours.
We get the job done. We know the drill by heart.
We press and fold the linen before it is loaded onto trucks,
Bound for back doors across the city.

ONE RAW FALL

Busted knuckles and a broken harp.
Seven storms in the past nine weeks.
He rents a crummy room two floors above the cab stand.
The only women on this street are married or impossible to reach.
Like wired dogs, boys race cars on the far bank boulevard.
He bandages his hand, leans into a foreign love song.
Last night he dreamt that he was in a carpenter's shop
With a lady judge who was explaining the science of joinery.

JIMMY ALLEN AT THE LIBRARY OF CONGRESS

The folklore researchers, all Ph.D.'s,
Dropped by to collect softball behavior,
Part of the Lowell Folklife Project.
Dr. Tom began shooting in the hot, low sun,
Backlighting trees at Parker Field;
Dr. Doug and Dr. Dave taped the chatter:
"C'mon now, be a hitter! Make the pitcher work."
After the win, Dr. Tom set up a team portrait,
Then everyone drove to the Civic Club
For a feast of popcorn, pizza, and beer.
Somebody kept yelling a cousin curse;
Dr. Tom made a note of the term.
Bird informed the bar regulars that
The folklore guys were "Congressmen,
Right from the Library of Congress!"
Frenchy and Dr. Dave sang "O, Canada"
While Dr. Tom took another team photo,
Sort of a "before and wasted" situation.
That's when we called it a night.
Months later, Dr. Doug gave a lecture
With slides on Capitol Hill for the erudite,
Including Smithsonian scholars and Geographic Society.
He showed a Greek priest, Cambodian dancers,
Skateboard kids, a wine-maker, and suddenly
Jimmy Allen was on the mound
In his crimson Burgess Construction jersey,
As big as he'd want to be on screen,
Throwing a strike for American folklife.

Parlez-vous?

Pierre Bouchard's sports-talk radio show
Finds its way from Montreal to my room,
The chatty French fading in and out;
I'm picking up key words, leaning towards
The Panasonic Solid-State portable.
In the dark I reached over to fine-tune
A Boston station and on the signal's edge
Caught a Canadian phone call in mid-flight—
The cold, clear December air a blue net,
The stars like a connect-the-dots game
Transmitting my root tongue,
Language of those who carried my name down
And down through Quebec backwoods, villages,
Down through pine cone valleys
To this mill town whose brick factories
Make a great red wall along the river.
Bouchard and his callers talk football, hockey;
A commercial praises lovely Montreal,
Paris of North America, cosmopolitan hive.
They wish each other "Joyeux Noël,"
Voices blinking slowly like fancy tree lights.

THE CHEST-PANTS BROTHERS

Crossing the lunch room to a perch near the guard shack,
Ricky and Skippy Lachance ran an alley of flak every day.
Hip-less at 21, they tugged trousers up under their arms.
They yakked about ferndocks and franistans,
About Tortilla the Hun and Lime Eddie.
A couple of Adams, they named each and all,
Not with any crooked aim, but to prove their punch.
Hunched in the corner, the twins riffed on news and notes,
Crafting their routine—bulking up on retorts.

Harry at the Lowell Conference

He kept telling us he dropped out of high school, but Harry spoke as well as any old politician at a hotel banquet. He asked why the U.S.A. and South Africa are the only modern countries without national health care. He called Reagan "a turkey" and described a White House full of smoky mirrors. Harry Callahan of the Industrial Workers said Nancy's idea of cruel and unusual punishment is being dragged to Sears and forced to pick a dress off the rack.

Harry isn't sure Labor should be a political party, but won't rule it out. "We're like rats," he said, "and when cornered, we'll fight—fight dirty if needed." Harry went to the Soviet Union. He said they have hearts and put pants on the same way we do. "Why shouldn't I go to learn something? The Pepsi and Caterpillar executives go twice a month." He wonders why Americans don't know history. He said most people want to be in unions, but aren't—people can see that union workers make more a week.

Harry said, "The democracy has problems. There's no democracy at work—never has been. American businessmen want authoritarian systems at work." He said he might be the first guy to put a bullet between the eyes of a capitalist if the fight goes to the street. He tells that to businessmen, he said, and they listen, confident that it will never happen.

1986

Manny and Maria

For the promised taste of handmade wine, I step into
Manny and Maria's cellar, lugging two bags of prizes
From a tour of their homey garden, with tomato plant
Stalks like broom handles and cukes so dense I could barely
Step between. A plum tree's laden branches brush grass tips,
And on one apple tree five varieties pop off stems.
Only the peach tree is empty—its spotted drops below.
And ten thousand grapes ripening. Marigolds, impatiens,
Dahlias, rose of Sharon along the chain fence.
All this in a side yard, no country acre, a plot someone else
Would mow and clip. Their news is lost on reporters,
This success beyond cameramen who fish for color.
The secret my wine-tricked tongue can spill is that this place
Is full of Mannys and Marias—their properties bursting
With melons, zinnias and zucchini, cherries and figs,
Ranks of native corn, rainbow sprays on sills, bathtub Madonnas
In white-rock shrines. Manny neatly tips a light-green bottle
To keep sediment in, his own California wine,
From grapes trucked to a corner Portuguese market
For local makers like himself who bottle this one he pulled
From the rack—so dry the ice barely sweats in my drained glass.

BETWEEN TWO WORLDS

Katherine O'Donnell Murphy, saver and giver—
Her "small oil painting" bought from the artist in Spring 1924,
Fresh from the Public Garden where he liked to sketch
And that day painted in oil Boston's Park Street Church—
Bought the work from him when he returned to his studio
At the New School of Design where Katherine was a student, too.
She would later lend it to the Whitney Museum and Washington
    Gallery (1962).
With fountain pen she wrote in the exhibition catalogue,
"It has been in my home since then, a reminder of my carefree days"—
Small lavender-toned scene purchased from the artist,
Dressed that day in a worn tweed jacket at the school
"Where Arshile Gorky and I were both students," she tells in blue ink
In the same hand as in another note quoting Hilton Kramer on Gorky
    in 1969:
"He was between two worlds, the European and American"—
Half-sheet tucked in the catalogue conveyed to the Lowell Art
    Association,
Along with the oil she bought from the tall man with curly black hair,
A gift in the U.S. Bicentennial year, artwork by an Armenian immigrant
    who,
In 1946, saw eight of his paintings and two of his drawings
Picked for a major-league show titled *Fourteen Americans*—this artist,
Who, having buried slain cousins, left his village in 1920 for New York,
Then Boston and Watertown Mass.—he studied at RISD,
Providence Tech, and Boston's New School of Design,
Where Lowell's Katherine O'Donnell got the painting one spring day,
Took it from his wide field-worker's hands,
Same hands he used to hang himself—after a barn fire ate 27 of his
    paintings,

After cancer, after the car crash in which he broke his neck,
After the rack of love—but on that spring day he was satisfied with the
     day's picture,
A painting later borrowed for a 1980 Guggenheim retrospective that
     traveled—
Dallas, Los Angeles County, and then back to Lowell—
A small oil, *Park Street Church, Boston*, the "little impressionist
     cityscape,"
So unlike the long free lines and morphology of his signal compositions,
This early scene bought from Gorky by a fellow student,
Who hung it in her house and followed his trajectory.

TSONGAS STEEL

"I view my approach as compassionate realism. Can you imagine a bumper sticker with those words on it?"

—Paul Tsongas (1941-1997)

1.

It's January in California. I tear open a package
Stuffed with birthday shirts, pistachios from Market Street,
And two-week-old *Sun*s telling of Paul Tsongas leaving the Senate.
Headlines had crossed the country: bulletins on Larry King's show,
Clip on *McNeil-Lehrer*, Ellen Goodman's column in the L.A. *Times*
About a sick father who sorted out kinds of ambition.
The hometown paper is epic—former staffers reacting,
Greek restaurant victory scenes, pictures of Paul in Israel,
With big Tip and Ted in Washington, and a family portrait.
Each summer the Merrimack River eases through the valley,
Spills over the dam, thins out, sneaks between rocks,
Then emerges whole in a wide, quiet metal-flake basin,
Right up against the city, in no hurry for the ocean.

1984

2.

Four huge flatbeds, flanked by cruisers with looping blue lights,
Slide through the intersection of Broadway and Dutton,
Hauling beams for the city's new arena named for Paul.
I see this on leaving his funeral service in a Byzantine geode,
Transfiguration Greek Orthodox Church—
Church of Metamorphosis, Church of Sudden Radiance,
Church of Radical Development, Church of Holy Light.
He's gone to the air, gone to the sun, gone to the waters, gone to the ground.
Who planned this steel motorcade just as mourners turned from the church?
Or was it perfect luck or chance or fate?
We know him well enough to say he would love
The idea of excellence in a steel embrace.

1997

ONE NIGHT

The good way
Don turned his
head and dropped
three nickels
into the bent
tambourine of
the Salvation
Army-man between
sips of 25-cent draft
and bites of pretzel
at the Old Worthen
in one of the high-
backed booths with
his three friends who
had stopped the cribbage
game when the deaf
Frenchman in a
blue-green overcoat
came to the table
with eyes of a
saint and handsome
brown gloves that
held the jingling
pan so our good
Christmas will
would get us to
push a few coins
his ever-loving way.

VALENTINE

Red sweater
Slim frame
Warm breast
Open-hearted
Look of her
On the train
Opposite me
World passes
World happens
Looking into
Each other—
Her sweater
Her shiny hair
Bright heat of it
Soft wool of it
Put my face
Right there
Right now

Rings of Saturn

Standing on the oval track, Jim Casselton and I studied the three-quarter moon in the soft blue sky, the dents and heights making a mottled milky surface that was papery in its translucence, as if the rock of a moon held its place as neatly as a shape cut out of a blank sheet. Way beyond, after seven years of transit over two billion miles, the latest celebrity spacecraft, *Cassini-Huygens*, was perambulating Saturn, having deked its way between swirling rings of ice chunks and universal gravel—sending back photographs of Saturnine moons like a tourist. But instead of a loud shirt and plaid shorts, a familiar flag logo adorns the underside, shielded as much as possible from the elements on the extreme ride. Jim said, "That moon seems especially large. And there's something odd about the light." A muscular man who stands about five-feet-eight-inches, he wore a Patriots sweatshirt, the one from the second Super Bowl win. When he saw me, he pointed to his blue cap and then to my Oakland A's cap, and said, "Tonight," meaning the A's would be playing the Red Sox at Fenway Park. He lives in "the housing" near the Common, a complex named for a local priest who became a bishop. He's usually finished with his workout before I arrive. Underfoot were dozens of spent red and blue casings of fireworks from last Sunday's Fourth of July celebration. "I had my windows open and heard them until all hours. It's not as tough as it used to be here. Summer carnivals were stopped after a guy got stabbed years ago. You have to keep your eyes open." He knows about incidents, being retired from the county sheriff's office. "In my sheriff years, a bunch of us would run in South Lowell on weekends. When I came to Lowell from Florida in 1959, that area was run down. It still has some inner-city problems, but look at the grapevines and fruit trees. People are keeping up appearances. Did you know Mr. Homer, the fisherman? He'd come around with his truck to the section where a lot of the black families lived and put out tubs of fish on ice, all kinds. He'd say to my mother,

'Go ahead, Mrs. Casselton, take a couple more. There are plenty in the ocean.'"

2004

"Failure of Imagination"
(*Christian Science Monitor*, Found Poem)

June 22, 2004.
Wide Iraqi support for Saddam's trial.
Democrats hope to retake South.
Iraqi rebels dividing, losing support.
Both big parties solidify swiftly.
Rumblings of war in heart of Africa.
Ranks breaking over North Korea.
Gender, work, and Wall Street.
Early signs of a "values" campaign.
In charge, Iraqis crack down hard.
Can spy agencies work together?
The election that won't budge.
Terror detainees win right to sue.
U.S. military lowers profile in Iraq.
Anti-Iran sentiment hardening fast.
"Failure of imagination" led to 9/11.
July 23, 2004

Ready to Go

The hooded young look like monks on the overpass.
I'm driving to the Park Center to see a film about forgotten artists.
My neighbor George stops near me at a signal light.
Back home, he wrote a "Motoring Column" for *The Nigerian Express*
Until he exposed a bidding-scandal tied to government cars.
Now he works in the Acre Laundry for the boss who threw me out
After I walked in and began to load clothes into a dryer.
"You wash here, too, or you go!" "But my machine broke," I squawked.
The Laundry sign is ahead when I blend into downtown traffic.
Today's newspaper gave us a lot on President-elect Obama.
It took a storm of will to change the political drift.
The kid-monks stream to the Common for a street-peace rally,
Hopping over doves stenciled on a sidewalk near the Owl Diner.
Golden vines grip the dented roadside fence.

"Beast Underneath"

I wake up early every day, but today I got up even earlier to check on our young cat that came home from the vet's late yesterday after being spayed. We were told to watch her closely for several days to be sure she is recovering as expected. I was awake, listening to New Hampshire Public Radio's station in Nashua with its overnight broadcast of the BBC World Service, when I heard the rattle of cans and cart wheels on the street through the open window. It was barely first light, but a middle-aged couple was making the rounds on trash pick-up day. They fished in the recycle bin for redeemable containers. A tall, thin older guy jogged past them on his way toward the courthouse. He was alone, but there are guys the same age as him who run this route in a group, probably jumping off from the "Y" on Thorndike Street. The clock read 4:32. Big cities like New York and Boston come to mind when you think about cities that don't sleep, but Lowell has its own 24/7 tempo—ask any police officer about the night rhythm. This time of year the birds keep time in the trees. Their music rises with the light.

The news as usual these days was angled toward war and money and politics. The Republic of Congo is marking its 50th year of independence from Belgium. Chaos and brutality have dominated the nation for five decades. At one point, ten African nations were fighting with and against political factions in Congo in what was called "Africa's World War." I also heard a report about Hamid Ismailov, an Uzbek novelist and poet from Kyrgyzstan now living in London. He's a writer-in-residence for the BBC who has been blogging about the turmoil in his homeland, where the Kyrgyz are fighting with people with roots in Uzbekistan who live in Kyrgyzstan. Listening to him, I was reminded of my friend Steve talking about the Irish Civil War and the more recent indiscriminate bombings when he was studying at Trinity College. Ismailov was asked if he was losing his faith in human nature, given all the violence. About the inter-ethnic strife in his homeland, he said, "I felt as if my hands were cutting my legs." He had written on his blog, "Are the crows who do not peck out each other's eyes more human than us?" and "Is civilization as thin as the shirt we wear, covering a beast underneath?" He said the stories of human kindness coming out of the war zones keep him hopeful.

Last week, a nineteen-year-old man from downriver in Lawrence was shot dead in the Back Central neighborhood, three blocks from my house. Juan Ferrer's death was a front-page news story. Two days after the shooting yellow police tape lay on the pavement in the alley where he was killed. He had been with friends at a barbeque, according to a news report. A black kettle-top grill stood in the alley. Dark curtains blew in an open window above. I asked a neighbor who knew him what happened. There was an argument. Somebody had a gun.

BLACK HOLE STREET

The main black hole in our galaxy is thirty times the size of our Sun. I made a note of that in 2000. There's an economic black hole ten years later. Some country singer cries, "They're shuttin' Dee-troit down." An optimist says 92 percent of adults have jobs, but that isn't even accurate. The closest black hole is 1,600 light-years into space. The local Career Center lines circle the block near St. Joseph the Worker Catholic shrine. So many shelves at the food bank are bare by mid-week. Can you tally a billion years on the back of a weekly paycheck? Neil Young yells, "Where did all the money go? Where did all the cash flow?" Is there a black hole in Dubai or a sinkhole in Palm Beach? A hot-gas halo loops the Milky Way, smoke from a vast erupted star. This place has been exploding for eons. Will the Kepler spacecraft find another planet that's just right?

Notes

"NASA launched a telescope Friday night that will search a slice of the Milky Way galaxy for Earth-like planets. The mission attacks a basic human question, according to NASA Associate Administrator Ed Weiler: "Are we alone?" The Kepler spacecraft carries a telescope that will stare at 100,000 stars in the Cygnus-Lyra region of the Milky Way for more than three years."
—CNN, *March 6, 2009, 10.59 p.m.*

Forty-six-year-old machine toolmaker Kim Allgeyer of Westland, Michigan, lost his job in January. He asked, "Who's going to put me to work? Where's the work at? It's just a great big black hole."
—The New York Times, *March 7, 2009*

On September 29, 2010, astronomers announced that they had identified an "Earthlike planet" in the Milky Way that they named Gliese 581g, which "sits smack in the middle of the so-called habitable zone orbiting at just the right distance from the star to let water remain liquid rather than freezing solid or boiling away. As far as we know, that's the minimum requirement for the presence of life. ... 'I think they've scooped the Kepler people,' scientist James Kasting said."
—www.time.com, *September 29, 2010*

five

CUT FROM AMERICAN CLOTH

IN THE MIDDLE OF THE NINETEENTH CENTURY, workers in the red-brick mills of Lowell, Massachusetts, each year produced enough cotton cloth to wrap the world. More importantly, the city known for manufacturing textiles produced the stuff of America itself: ideas and merchandise, entrepreneurs and generals, politicians and artists, religious leaders and labor champions, sports heroes and movie stars, inventors and criminals, and a multitude of citizens from the immigrants, refugees, and migrants who crowded its streets.

To understand America, a good place to start is where you are. In my case it is Meetinghouse Hill, the rise on the far side of the South Common opposite my house. With my wife and son, I live at 44 Highland Street in Lowell. In 1880, my great-great grandfather Marion trekked from Canada to find work in this burgeoning northeast Massachusetts mill city, and I was born in a neighborhood across the river nine years after my father returned from World War II. Like my father's people, my mother's ancestors traveled the Normandy-Quebec-Lowell route. My wife's heritage is Irish on both sides, with Lowell roots winding back to the 1870s. Our son is named for the original Marion in Lowell, a carpenter, and her grandfather, a longtime jeweler in the city—all Josephs.

Built in 1860s, my family's house was once owned by the Appleton Manufacturing Company, which was formed in 1828, five years after the first mill began producing cloth in Lowell. The Appleton's managers who lived in the house through the late nineteenth century could see the tops of their factories from the second floor windows. Our house was bought in the 1930s by my wife Rosemary's grandparents, the jeweler Joseph Foley and his wife, Gertrude O'Neill Foley. Joe Foley's mother scrubbed floors and washed dishes in the mansion at 42–44 Highland Street not long after she emigrated from Ireland. Imagine the satisfaction and sense of class revenge in Joe's heart as he signed the purchase papers.

On special occasions, when we sit for dinner in our elaborately detailed front room, I picture a scene in *Doctor Zhivago*, the one in which the poet-physician returns to Moscow from his forced service with fighters in the hinterlands only to see that the Bolsheviks have confiscated his family's house. When he looks up at the scruffy crowd hanging over the upstairs banister and asks what is going on, one of the comrades tells him the arrangement is "more just." In the moment all he can do is agree. "Yes, more just."

From my bedroom window, I look across the Common to the red-brick Eliot Presbyterian Church atop Meetinghouse Hill. In 1930, the Massachusetts Bay Colony Tercentenary Commission installed a bronze plaque near the church, marking the location of Reverend John Eliot's log cabin chapel in 1648. Adventurer Simon Willard, who had clashed with local peoples since arriving in the colony, built the cabin to use as a frontier court—it was the first structure built by Anglo settlers in the place that became Lowell.

A graduate of Jesus College of Cambridge, Eliot started out as a school assistant in Chelmsford, England. After converting to Puritanism, he fled to Massachusetts in 1631 to avoid persecution. Eliot was the first Christian preacher to journey from Boston to the village of Wamesit, named for its tribe, at the confluence of the Merrimack and Concord rivers. Beginning with a first trip to the northwest woods in 1647, Eliot often traveled with Major General Daniel Gookin, Superintendent of Indians in the colony, who "saved Eliot's neck more than once," wrote Rev. David Malone, former pastor of the Eliot Church.

In 1653, colonial officials designated the broad wedge of land bounded by the Concord and Merrimack for the Pennacook peoples—to be their property. Everything around them had already been signed away by Passaconaway, leader of the local tribes who has come down to us through European accounts as a shaman who could set water aflame, generate a live snake by rubbing its shed skin in his hands, and make trees vibrate. Passaconaway deeded to the English a vast tract of land between present-day Newburyport, Massachusetts, and the Merrimack River. Fifteen years later, he committed his people to the governance of the Bay Colony. His strategy of accommodation hardly satisfied the settlers' appetite for land and control. By 1660, the English had moved deep into the interior, and all evidence suggested more of them were coming. Passaconaway gathered his people for a farewell address—the substance of which was reported by an English observer with partial understanding of Algonkian. "I am going the way of all the earth," the sachem began.

"I am ready to die and not likely to see you met together anymore. . . . Take heed how you quarrel with the English. Hearken to the last words of your father and your friend. The white men are the sons of the morning. The Great Spirit is their father. . . . Never make war with them. Sure as you light the fires, the breath of heaven will turn the flame upon you and destroy you . . . ."

According to legend, Passaconaway withdrew to the northern mountains and some years later was swept into the sky in a huge maple sleigh drawn by flying gray wolves.

The area to the right of my house steps down to the western bank of the Concord and until recent times was called Wamesit Hill, though the only Native American in sight is the one positioned at the center of the state emblem that appears on the Tercentenary plaque on Meetinghouse Hill and on the flag of the Commonwealth of Massachusetts displayed outside the Superior Court House nearby and at the Gallagher Transportation Center a block away.

In the early winter of 1943, twenty-year-old Jack Kerouac had a night job parking cars at the Hotel Garage on Middlesex Street, on the back slope of Meetinghouse Hill. He was in sight of a handsome brownstone train depot, since demolished, a short way up the tracks from Gallagher terminal. Long before he composed his signature "October in the Railroad Earth," he sketched the local scene during down time in the garage office, itself now gone:

"One night, returning from work in the casual, squalid atmosphere of railroad yards, warehouses, switch towers, idle boxcars, and one lonely little lunch cart across the tracks, as I was approaching the rail crossing near the old depot that we have in my home town, I had to lean against a sagging fence (black with soot-years) for fully ten minutes while a mighty locomotive went by freighting ninety-six cars: coal cars, oil tanks, wooden boxcars, all types of commercial rolling stock. While I loafed there with a cigarette, watching each car rumble past and checking the cargoes, a thought came to me with swift and lucid impact, with the same jolt of common sense and disbelief in the scantiness of my own intelligence that I had felt when first I understood the working of a mathematic equation. 'Why,' I asked myself, 'does not this rich cargo, these cars, that terrific locomotive belong to me? . . . and to my fellow men? . . . Why are they not, like my trousers, my property? Who covets these great things so that myself and my fellow men are not heir to their full use?' Then I asked myself, 'Are we not all men living alone on a single earth?'"

The morning freight train slides behind the long red flank of a former patent medicine lab and continues past the terminal while passengers wait for the 9:07 a.m. run to Boston. Copper flashing gleams on the adjacent roof of gray granite Keith Academy, once the turreted city jail and since renovated into upscale apartments. The boxcars are blocks of American place. Appalachicola, Port St. Joe Route, Soo Line, Maine Central, Rio Grande, Milwaukee, Santa Fe, Illinois Terminal, Penn Central, Southern Pacific, Bangor and Aroostook, Atlantic and Western, Boston and Maine—national freight, movable goods, raw material, made things—the weight that spreads cross country. Everything seems to come through Lowell. Burlington Northern, Springfield Terminal, Canadian Pacific.

What happened to the Canadian Sausage Company of Lowell? The red-and-white trucks scooted around the city, delivering fresh meats to grocers and butchers. Like the freight cars of place, the sausage trucks stood for the French-Canadian presence. If you were French Canadian, you noticed when the truck passed by. You saw that word "Canadian."

It was like seeing maple leaf cookie packages in the crackers-and-cookies aisle at the market. And it made you think of grandparents, who served plates of maple leaf cookies and offered Christmastime gift boxes of painfully sweet, grainy, creamy maple candies.

On a siding just north of the station, there's a scrap train—ground-up fenders and stoves and corroded pipes en route to the smelter, the chopped ham of American industry. In the rail yard, freight-car murals in graffiti code, the blocky colored letters like harsh plastic alphabet-magnets on a refrigerator door.

Next to the train station stands the ugly mill building on Thorndike Street that you cannot miss, if you listen to local cable TV commercials from Comfort Furniture. The wavy wooden floors of the five-story complex creak and squeak when customers wind through aisles between the tons of sofas, recliners, dining room sets, lamps of all types, coffee tables, bunk beds with matching desks, and assembly-required home entertainment center shelf units. There is only a hint of the patent medicine production plant that thrived in this factory. Running sideways up the tapered brick chimney is the word "Hood's," for C.I. Hood & Company, one of the city's two massive patent medicine operations of the nineteenth century. Cartons of vegetable pills, tooth powder, olive ointment, and syrups promising cures for everything from rheumatism to syphilis filled the loading dock. When it was built in 1893, the Hood laboratory was the world's largest medicine manufacturing building. Charles Hood's specialty was a bottled syrup called Sarsaparilla, which promised to "cure neuralgia pains."

Lowell's patent medicine firms helped shape the future of not only entrepreneurship, but also mass advertising in this country. Pill-making and bottling plants were combined with on-site printing shops. Hood's main competitor in Lowell was J.C. Ayer & Company, which, at its height around 1900, published promotional literature, especially *American Almanac*, in various languages around the world—fifteen million copies. Master salesman Ayer showered emperors, pashas, and even the Czar of Russia with fancy cartons of his Cherry Pectoral respiratory elixir. The medicine industry picked up some of the business slack when textile manufacturing sagged. One of its lasting effects is that people in this region still ask for a "tonic" when ordering a soft drink. Outside the office, on the second floor of Comfort Furniture, the owners have a display of colorized postcards, a "Sarsaparilla Rainy Day Puzzle," and crinkled photographs from the Hood firm.

For the first seventeen years that I lived on Highland Street, every weekday at 3 p.m. during the school year a dozen or more yellow buses pulled into the semi-oval driveway in front of the Rogers Middle School that faces my house. The school was a microcosm of New Lowell, with Cambodian-Americans making up more than half the building's population—the rest were Portuguese-American kids from long-settled families around St. Anthony's parish in the Back Central section and newcomers from Brazil, Cameroon, and Guatemala, along with the third-, fourth-, fifth-, or sixth-generation Lithuanian-, Greek-, French Canadian-, and Irish-American youngsters. The descendants of the native peoples and early English colonists are as scarce as heirloom species in the flower boxes under the windows on Elm Street a block away. In the school lobby students with newcomer DNA could read about Edith Nourse Rogers, who still holds the record as the woman who served longest without interruption in the U.S. House of Representatives (1925 – 1960). The Great Recession of 2008-09 claimed the Rogers as City Hall budget cuts led to its closing—despite the "Rogers School Rocks" protest signs waved by kids and their parents.

"Congresswoman Rogers was a liberal and an internationalist," writes Mary H. Blewett, longtime professor of history at the University of Massachusetts–Lowell, "typical of successful Republicans of the northeast. She voted for most of the key New Deal programs of the thirties—the Wagner Act which protected union organization, the Social Security Act of 1935, and the minimum wage law of 1938—in line with the needs of her Lowell constituents, if not with the Republican leadership."

A Mainer by birth, Rogers married into a wealthy textile industry family in Lowell, where she had studied in a private girls' school. She succeeded her husband, Congressman John Rogers, when he died in office. "Mrs. Rogers" became the veterans' best friend, her experience with the military having begun with agencies serving the wounded in France during World War I. In 1939, moved by reports of abuse of German Jews, especially the brutality of *Kristallnacht* (the sanctioned night attack on Jews in their homes, shops, and synagogues), she and Sen. Robert F. Wagner of New York filed a refugee aid bill that would have allowed 20,000 German refugee children into the United States. President Franklin D. Roosevelt withheld his support, and despite lobbying by children's advocates across America, the bill was defeated at the committee level. Mrs. Rogers backed laws creating a Women's Army Auxiliary Corps in 1941 and the G.I. Bill of Rights, the latter providing a range of social, financial, and educational benefits to World War II veterans. She was seventy-nine when she died in 1960, in the midst of a re-election campaign.

Mrs. Rogers was in the middle of a line of Republican U.S. Representatives from the Lowell area who controlled the seat from 1859 to 1974, with the exception of a single two-year term for Democrat John K. Tarbox (1875 – 1877). It took a man who grew up on Highland Street to break the Republican streak.

Sitting at a desk in his father's dry-cleaning shop on Gorham Street in June 1968, just days after Senator Robert Kennedy was assassinated, twenty-seven-year-old Paul Tsongas wrote a letter to the editor of the *Lowell Sun*:

"I read with dismay your editorial attacking foreign reaction to the tragedy of Robert Kennedy. Your advice for them to 'keep their stupid mouth shut' is not the kind of reasoned awareness for which these times call. No one has much patience with those who allege conspiracy in the murders of President Kennedy, Medgar Evers, Martin Luther King, Robert Kennedy, and whoever should follow them. Certainly many foreign capitals wish us ill and will resort to misrepresentations. This however should not obscure the fact that the world beyond our borders, including our closest friends, stands horrified at our shoot-em-up mentality.

"I was in a small village in Ethiopia with the Peace Corps when President Kennedy was slain. My grief and agony were shared by the Ethiopians among whom I lived. They shed tears over the senseless death of such a 'Tru Sew' (good man). They felt that he belonged to the world and the promise of a brotherhood, and his death did indeed diminish us all. This was at the time when *Time* magazine would arrive with graphic pictures of Bull Conner and his dogs brutalizing Southern blacks. We did what we could to defend America. It became very difficult when four of my Ethiopian students came to the United States and received the stinging backlash of racism. They returned to Ethiopia forever disillusioned with a nation that professes to believe that 'all men are created equal.'"

The next year he won a seat on the Lowell City Council and set out on his own "journey of purpose," to quote the title of a book of his speeches and essays.

He and his fellow Democratic members of the "Watergate Class" dominated the 1974 election and took office the following January with a mandate to reform the government. The son of a Harvard-educated small-businessman, Tsongas was raised in a large white house on the corner of Highland and Thorndike streets. He caught the public service fever from President John F. Kennedy and, ultimately, as a former U.S. Senator challenged Arkansas Governor Bill Clinton one-on-one in the 1992 presidential primaries, winning New Hampshire and eight more state contests before an empty war chest forced him to withdraw. Through his Washington years he had a red-phone connection to Lowell's City Hall and made the city's rebirth his passion. It became an article of faith with him that one must honor the toil of past generations and respect the potential of future generations.

The reclaiming of Lowell came to symbolize that faith. Tsongas embodied the "Don't Quit" character of Lowell that explains in part the community's resurgence. He wrote the legislation that created Lowell National Historical Park in 1978, adding his hometown to the list that includes the Grand Canyon and Statue of Liberty. The cradle of the American Industrial Revolution would be preserved. The renaissance sparked by the park made Lowell a model of urban regeneration. In the last thirteen years of his life he was as well known for his high-profile fight against cancer. He died of pneumonia in 1997.

Places change, people enter and exit the stage—we won't see Paul Tsongas jogging through the South Common, we won't see Brother Gilbert who taught at Keith Academy after mentoring the young sportsman George Herman Ruth (the "Babe") in Baltimore or Ruth Meehan who organized U.S.O. shows around the world and drove a candy apple-red coupe out of the driveway at 48 Highland.

Some buildings are lost entirely. The Commodore Ballroom, later Mr. C's Rock Palace, once commanded the middle of Thorndike Street. The big bands and blues greats made it the favored nightspot. In the '60s, major acts like Paul Revere and the Raiders and local phenoms like Little John and the Sherwoods headlined on weekends. You have to find it in pictures on the web now.

Somewhere in my local travels I heard a story about Jim Morrison of The Doors arriving early for a gig at the Commodore in the fall of 1967 when "Light My Fire" was still torching the competition. He had heard Kerouac was living on Sanders Avenue, about five minutes away by car, so he got a ride over to see the forty-five-year-old author who by all accounts was in serious physical decline. When he got to the house, Mrs. Kerouac refused to let him in. Ragged young visitors materialized on the doorstep all the time. There would be no grand encounter of bare-chested pop poet and booze-bellied Beat Pop. Jack was sleeping.

From my front porch, I can take in the site of Simon Willard's court at Wamesit Village and the present Superior Court of the county, where Daniel Webster argued cases and then stayed for dinner. With St.

Peter Church razed, only one of Highland Street's great gray bookends remains, the sturdy Lowell Jail that became a Catholic High School for boys—which, to some graduates, was not a substantial change of use at all. On mornings when I circle the track at the bottom of the Common's green bowl, I scan a roster of names tied to the ridgeline of buildings— Rev. Eliot, politico Charles Gallagher, Hood the Medicine Man, theatre-magnate Keith of the Academy, and Congresswoman Rogers.

These names are entwined in history like the signature grapevines of the neighborhood, hundreds of them planted through the decades by Portuguese immigrants—green signs marking the presence of people who turn open space around their modest homes into miniature farms along the narrow, hilly ways. In the right season, waiting a minute before starting their cars for the drive to work, my neighbors, gardeners like Joe Veiga and Natalie Silva, hear the larks and the locomotive pulling toward Boston.

2012

six

The War Place (1. and 2.)
War of the Settlers and Natives and The War of Independence

War of the Settlers and Natives

Part One

"On the morning of March 18, 1676,
In crossing the river in a boat
With two of his sons and his daughter,
To milk the cows, with a squad of soldiers,
The Indians fired upon them as the boat struck the shore,
And killed the two sons who were at the oars.
One fell back into his sister's lap.
The soldiers were so alarmed
As not to fire until called upon
By the father who fired and called out,
'Do not let dead men be at the oars.'
They were buried in Howard's Field near the river.
The Indians fled, and it was uncertain
Whether any of them were killed or not."

PART TWO

"In 1725, when he was twenty-one years of age,
He joined the company commanded by Capt. John Lovewell,
Which went to Pigwackett, now Fryeburg, Maine,
On snow shoes to hunt for Indians.
They surprised and killed a party
Consisting of nine Indians and a boy.
These they scalped in order to get the bounty
Then offered by the Bay State Colony for evidence of slaughter.
For this prowess, he, with the command,
Received the thanks of the General Court,
And an award as the law provided."

The War of Independence

Part One

Late July 1776, "Marched for Cannada" from Dracut
"to Chelmsford to Westford
to Groton to Pepperal
to Ashby to Ashbinham
to New Ypswich to Ringe
to Jaffrey to New Molbury
to Swansey to Keen to Surry
to Westmoreland to Walpole to Charlestown N.H.
to Springfield to Wethirsfield
to Cavendish to Saltish
to Ludlow to Sasbury to Clarodin
to Rutland to Caselton
to Skeensborough
to Mount Independence
to Ticonderoga
October ye 5 1776"

Part Two

August.
Isaac, Asa, Elijah, Zachariah,
all carried down to the lake
"sick with the small pox."
I worked in camp.
September.
News of fighting in New York. 2,000 dead.
One night a rumor of spies,
so we kept to our tents and watched.
October.
Guard duty. We cleaned our pieces,
expecting the King's troops.
The last Sunday, enemy boats landed—
"We fired 2 Cannon from ye Sandy Redout
and heard we killed some men."
November.
Hunting with 2 sergeants, I killed a buck.
One night we had a very hot fire.
The 26th. A red-letter day. Left for Dracut.
Through Saratoga, Still Water, Half Moon,
meals of "Cyder, Bisket & Chees."
December.
At Albany, "Crost the River to Green Bush,"
then east across Massachusetts.
Bought a horse. Headed home.

Section 1 is drawn from the writings of the Varnum family of Dracut, Massachusetts, The Varnums of Dracut *by John M. Varnum (1907), whose ancestors arrived in Ipswich, Mass., in 1635. Section 2 includes passages from a diary kept by Micah Hildreth of Dracut in 1776. The source is* The History of Dracut *by Silas R. Coburn (1922). With his brothers William and Josiah, 26-year-old Micah joined Captain Peter Coburn's Dracut militiamen when they engaged British troops at Lexington, Mass., on April 19, 1775. He later fought at Bunker Hill and in the siege of Boston in late 1775.*

CARNIVAL ON THE DUMP

A huge white sign announces recovered earth.
The landfill nicks wetlands where marsh life steams.
The sealed dump one day will yield milk glass and ball bearings.
This April, a neon extravaganza occupies the site.
They say a sign in Georgia reads,
"Macon is the seventh layer of civilization on this spot."
The mound builders of 1000 A.D.—dust under the tobacco yards.
A luxurious Ferris Wheel and the red-eyed Octopus
Grind and loop to the tooting calliope music
Pumping in circles and dipping rhythm
Over the worms churning cardboard in their guts.

BUSH PILOTS

The pilot sprouted from the cockpit,
Lobbed backwards until silk puffed,
And his parachute, tiny mushroom,
Held in the wind over fir-crested woods.
Part of our Air Force hobbled out of the sky
Toward spears, where it caught,
And tangled wings and splintered fuselage
And cracked its nose cone as silver stars
Hit ground in a black-and-orange noise.

For years, we dug up traces of burnt metal,
Once thinking our relic was a helmet chip,
Rare as the fossil of St. Therese
Buried at our yellow-brick school.
We rummaged in the ruins for bits of wreck,
Not pieces of the Dream—that lure of pretty steel.
Like blue angels in a wild blue yonder,
We hitched our saintly wagons to a star,
But fumbled with the junk that fell around us.

Narratives in Plastic

Among the things I'd like to have back are my "little men," finger-sized colored figures of Roy Rogers, Davy Crockett, Robin Hood, and the green troopers of World War II. On my bedroom's hardwood floor, kneeling in sun sliced by Venetian blinds, I created narratives in plastic with soldiers, spacemen, horses, and trucks. There was even a set of small white Presidents, a cereal box offer—George Washington to Eisenhower. I had black-and-yellow pirates and red-and-green Indians. Foreign Legionnaires fought Arabs on camels. A blue woman holding a basket of eggs tended farm animals. Silver carbines fit into the grips of frozen marksmen who came alive with the story line. Brown cowboys had holes in their hands for six-guns. Horses of every size and shade were rounded up for a posse or cavalry charge.

On the flat world of the floor, History, a catalogue of conflict, played between the bed and bureau, from the radiator to the closet, new stories each morning, grand dramas in miniature: the skirmish, the attack, the rescue, ambushes, and invasions. Knights, Nazis, redcoats, Martians, any enemy would do to join the battle and the make-believe. The play was improvisation on a theme—skits giving voice to blue-sky inventions and figures from movies, TV, or the real. I spent hours daydreaming—time on my knees, on my butt, on my side—setting and moving the pieces until I was done or bored or sent to bed, and even then I'd find a few army guys stranded in the hills of my quilt. If I had them back, I'd know more of what I did and why. They'd be artifacts from ages four through twelve, when I was building my brain in the corner room.

SPACE LUNCHBOX

"In a nutshell, the universe is 13.7 billion years old, plus or minus one percent; a recent previous estimate had a margin of error three times as much. By weight it is four percent atoms, 23 percent dark matter—presumably undiscovered elementary particles left over from the Big Bang—and 73 percent dark energy. And it is geometrically 'flat,' meaning that parallel lines will not meet over cosmic scales. The result, the astronomers said, is a seamless and consistent history of the universe, from its first few seconds, when it was a sizzling soup of particles and energy, to the modern day and a sky beribboned with chains of pearly galaxies inhabited by at least one race of puzzled and ambitious bipeds."

—Dennis Overbye, writing about a map of the universe compiled by a satellite called the Wilkinson Microwave Anisotropy Probe, The New York Times, February 12, 2003

I CARRIED A BLUE METAL SPACE-THEMED lunchbox to school in the first grade at a wooden schoolhouse in a town whose Algonkian name means "A place in the woods." On my lunchbox were two Earth pilots wearing clear round helmets walking toward a rocket vehicle. Around the sides were illustrations of silver spaceships on an arid plain ringed by jagged hills over which shone a massive orange moon. It was a cartoon version of outer space, a vision from science fiction stories at a time when our idea of interplanetary travel was shaped by flying-saucer movies like *The Day the Earth Stood Still*, from 1951, introducing the mysterious Klaatu, a kind and stern spaceman, and his robot, Gort.

My teachers taught the basic subjects and good conduct. When the day was rainy or too cold for my classmates and me to go into the play yard for recess, we listened to phonograph records on a hand-cranked music-playing machine called a Victrola. We took turns requesting music. I usually picked "My Old Kentucky Home" by Stephen Foster. I don't know why other than I liked the melody. We didn't have Elvis, Little Richard, or even Jimmie Rogers in the stack of recordings, and anyway I didn't know rock and roll in the fall of 1959.

I probably heard the Russians had fired a metal orb named *Sputnik* into Earth orbit in 1957 and sparked what came to be known as the Space Race. An older friend of mine who was then in the Navy in Rhode Island saw tiny *Sputnik* low overhead in the gray dawn. Waiting with fellow sailors to march to breakfast, he heard buzzing, a whoosh as it passed. "That damn Russian spacecraft we had heard about was flying over us."

I would not have known that the National Aeronautics and Space Administration (NASA) of the United States had been formed in 1959 and that one of the first men recruited was Lt. Col. Alan B. Shepard, Jr., of Derry, New Hampshire, where Robert Frost had his first farm, but I certainly knew about Shepard in May 1961, when he shot into the clouds inside the *Freedom 7* capsule atop a Redstone rocket and landed in a ticker-tape parade in New York City draped in praise from our new young president, John F. Kennedy of Massachusetts. Shepard stayed with NASA long enough to hit golf balls on the moon.

I kept that blue metal space-themed lunchbox for years, later using it to store small plastic pill bottles filled with dimes and nickels from a coin collection. For me, in those days, Space as a concept meant the future. It was the next chapter of the American story. My father had fought in World War II, which was the previous big chapter. I was too young to grasp the happenings of the 1950s, from the bloody Korean War and racial strife to the Beat Generation writers. Unlike my father, who said the country slept for eight years under President Eisenhower, I liked Ike, war hero and grandfather, and stood with my glass of milk with the other "small fry" for the daily Toast to the President when "Big Brother" Bob Emery turned to the official portrait on the set of his Boston TV show.

My mind's eye opened for good around 1960. One of the first things I saw was space exploration. Through the early years of grammar school, each time an astronaut blasted into space or splashed down in the ocean, my class was allowed to watch the event on a television mounted on a tall wheeled cart in front of the room. The nation tracked those launches and recoveries. Kids may not have been able to pronounce the name of the Russian cosmonaut Yuri Gagarin, the first human to orbit the Earth, but we knew America and the Soviet Union were competing in "Can you top this?" The names of America's Project Mercury astronauts were as familiar to us as Rudolph's reindeer group—Scott Carpenter, Gordon Cooper, John Glenn, Gus Grissom, Wally Shirra, Alan Shepard, and Deke Slayton.

Soon we had the space story in bubble-gum pack trading cards on the variety store counter next to the baseball stars like Sandy Koufax and Willie Mays. In the late '50s, my brothers collected the first space cards with comic-book illustrations of a dog in a capsule, meteor showers, and men in protective gear frying eggs on the surface of Mercury. That set stepped its way to a moon landing and return, complete with imaginary flight-control centers and lunar greenhouses to feed a colony. The pictures on my cards came from color news photographs. I was in the future.

DUCHARMES' PORCH

Nineteen-sixty-six was the UFO summer in New Boston Village and Crosby Heights, the former being the lowland in my growing-up neighborhood and the latter the wooded incline being rapidly cleared for houses. Mr. and Mrs. Ducharme on Cinderella Circle sat on their back porch every summer night with binoculars and a solar system map watching for odd lights in the sky. Cinderella had been a frog-breeding swamp, Gendreau's Pond, filled in during the suburban land rush. Green leapers, languid in the heat, stretched their leopard-dot thighs behind them. Huge blue sewing-needles strafed us near algal water rife with hornpout and muskrats. That two adults made an observation post unnerved us on our Sting-Ray bikes cruising the loop of new, two-level homes in the long twilight after supper and obsessively checking in with the look-outs when the porch lights clicked on. One street over, unpaved, we poured sand on flaming signal pots and stepped into the whale-mouth bucket of a parked front-end loader. A name flew to us, a sing-song plea, "Eeeee-laine," someone's anxious mother calling in the dark.

The radio bled through the Ducharme kitchen window screen with a revved up talk-show host and callers re-hashing the latest news about the self-reported abduction of Betty and Barney Hill. The story had broken in a fast-selling book that was excerpted in the large-format *Look* magazine. The couple claimed to have been taken aboard a spaceship by lizard-eyed extraterrestrials wearing cadet caps who interrupted their homeward drive just south of the White Mountains in New Hampshire, a road I had traveled with my family. Under hypnosis the Hills described medical-type examinations both had been subjected to and recreated a map that suggested that the aliens may have zoomed to Earth from a star system thirty-seven light-years away, Zeta Reticuli. All this was gasoline to fire up twelve-year-old brains already fueled with pop culture space-lore on television, from spooky series like *The Outer Limits* and *Fantasmic Features* hosted by the lightbulb-headed creature-character Feep to the jokey adventures of the cartoon *Jetsons* and Space Family Robinson on *Lost in Space* (the more knowing science fiction of *Star Trek* premiered in September that year).

The Ducharmes and their older children jumped up and went to the railing facing south each time one of the parents called out about a streaking light over the cemetery a half-mile away. What's that? It's moving! They always swore they saw an orange blip inside the white dot.

LIME EDDIE

It's about naming something "something."
It's about high school, teen-age.
It's about making your own way,
Making your own words.
It's about Eddie's Ice Cream stand
Where we bought icy lime drinks.

PINE BROOK

One day I saw an old man in navy blue work pants, gray shirt, and a
green cap park his car near the condemned bridge on Phineas Street,
and then head down a path to the water's edge—a fisherman, I thought,
or a can collector. What did he think of me, atop a rock, writing in a
notebook while squirrels thrashed in the brilliant leaves? Acorns dropped
pop-pop-pop on asphalt. Three Canada geese patrolled the opposite
bank. Bulldozers over the ridge added a bass line to the brook's music.
Feathered seed fliers spilled from the lips of milkweed pods. Sun lit the
russet underbrush. Knuckled reeds looked like they had been lifted from
a Japanese print. Blue-black water rippled around glacial boulders. Down
a path there was a long-abandoned pale yellow foreign car with its guts
ripped out. Scratched on the hood were the names "Lee" and "Mel."
Electrical power lines ran up toward Ledge Hill's giant A-shaped rock
with the words "Fuckers Leap" in white paint—the high point where the
view-shed takes in our stretch of the river valley. Leaves let go like the last
flakes of October—one here, two there. The man kicked at a beer carton
in a thicket. He placed a red soda can in the trunk of his car and took out
a snow-brush to clean his pants.

Bottled Milk

Bothered by flies, a black calf rubs its head against a fence rail. Odors of grass, feed, and animals mix into one healthy country smell. Up the hill behind the barn a trail leads to a cemetery with many illegible stones, others with chiseled verse, and a few that read, "Gone Home." A dozen cars are notched in around the farm store. Here, not far from the city beat, I stand in the dirt and sense the natural loop, the closed circuit that runs from rain to bread, from clover to cheese. In a few months the farmer will set out hundreds of pumpkins for adoption by people who will place them on their front steps in descending order, the largest for the head of the household, smallest for the baby or cat. Pint-sized pumpkins will be given to third-grade teachers. Pies will feature the orange pulp. Then vines will be plowed under, Halloween torn from the calendar. And I'll step out of the store in the early darkness, holding a milk bottle by the neck in each hand like cold white lanterns.

Cattle Near Beaver Brook

Cattle wander to the barbed edge of the pasture,
Their scruffed autumn coats as thick as sofa stuffing.
White-faced large calm heads chew and stare at me.
A low sun slathers them in palomino light.

Swallows transmit themselves through air—
The wings pump silence. Glossy caucusing crows,
delegates from the corn lobby, break for their districts.
All at the same time, the cattle blink and turn.

THE WAR PLACE (12.)
9/11

On a rise on the south bank just below the rocky grill of the riverbed, students at his college carved into stone his name and those of six others from the school to remember John, who grew up to be a pilot and a farmer, who shared his land with Asian refugees who had resettled in the inner precincts of Lowell and who wanted to grow vegetables as they did in Cambodia, Vietnam, and Laos, a region from which John had flown home hurt soldiers in the closing years of the Vietnam War; John the preservationist, who saved open space in Dracut, called *Agumtoocook* by native people for its vast forest; John, who on September 11, 2001, lifted his passengers into a "severe clear" sky, nothing but blue on the route west; John, who guided American Airlines Flight 11 out of Boston's Logan Airport, where so many of us have flown away with faith in the promise of technology, management, and civilized behavior; John, who carried his travelers into boundless air on a day when he had as usual driven in early from Marsh Hill to captain his plane across country, that day like any other in the late summer, not officially fall even though schools were in session; that day like no other by the end of the morning, by the end of the paper rain and ash-cloud, by the end of the twisted steel and burnt ground, by the end of John's life—on that day from which we have not fully recovered the bounce that has always made people elsewhere admire our sure belief that Americans can figure out a problem and invent the next dazzle—a day that moved John's neighbors and even strangers to drive slowly up the winding hill road that leads to his farm, where they heaped flowers, handmade signs, candles, sympathy cards in front of the wide white gate leading to the farm, piled high the cut flowers, placed in silence—and past the white gate up the driveway a giant crane held an American flag that looked as big as the flag that covers the left field wall at Fenway Park on opening day—and past the crane and flag was the farmhouse of John's family, his wife and daughters, who needed him

to come back so he would sit next to them at the table in the house one
more time.

DESIRE LINES

At Runaway Hill where a horse broke wild
Flinging a preacher down the slope,
A stone wall links two chestnut trees and splits a field,
One half thick green, the other sun-burnt straw.
Meadows littered with glacial debris raise vines
That make rose hip jelly and blackberry jam.
Past rows of corn stubble, past crow woods
Where yellow maples and October oaks flamed,
Birds scatter above a pen of sooty pigs
Whose noses rub the gnawed turf.

Returning later in the year, I see blond weeds
Poking through snow scraps, patches in shadows
Near rusted firs and stands of birch, thick as my wrist.
Fields open onto beaver flats, all swamp and sedges.
The view shows marsh up to the high school gym,
And beyond its aqua panels, my first neighborhood,
Where my face was the center of the center of the universe,
Then way off, dim blue hills, far from the space of my past.
I like to stand on this rise and look out, look long,
Trying to imagine where I'll be looking back from later.

AT THE RED HOUSE

She crouches to get rough
with weeds.
Her scarecrow, Grace,
points stiff arms
at raiders
who'd wreck the corn.
The young woman
in white shorts and work boots
uses a jackknife
to cut suckers off tomato plants,
then pulls up
her jersey,
making a holder
for the green beans.

Show Me How to Float

Place a hand on my chest,
the other under me.
Teach me how to breathe.
"It's easy to float. Relax,
let your ears go underwater," she said.
And when my head goes back
and water rises in a circle
around chin and cheekbones,
I'll use your lesson,
and try to let go,
and test my strength,
trusting my body to take calm breaths.

Do You Think You'll Ever Go Back?

A cardinal on a phone line spilled sound into a hot sky.
Every Sunday morning, I cut through the woods to buy
The news at the variety store. Looking at me and tipping
His chin up, my father used to ask, "Do you think you'll
Ever go back?" A friend of mine says we can go back
To a place, but not back to a place in time.

At the town's edge, in Nifty Square, a woman asked me
What I was looking for. She said I was copying names
From mailboxes on a tenement next to Pete's Grain.
An old man fishing in Beaver Brook glanced at me
On the bridge. Leaves like large yellow postage stamps
Drifted into the reflection of fabulous trees.

Do I think I'll ever go back? My father didn't say "come back,"
As in the transmigration of souls. Do I want to go back?
It's like reading a book once—did I really get it all?
Was my father asking if I thought it was foolish or wondering
If I'd try? People pass away and trees grow taller,
But the song on the wire looks like the same bird.

OUR BODIES

The atoms
in our bodies
are old
exploded stars,
a cosmic alchemy,
still coming,
whispering past
shaggy galaxies,
where tunnels of blue soup
engulf crumbs of light.

Author's Note

Paul Marion is the author of several collections of poetry including *What Is the City?* and editor of *Atop an Underwood: Early Stories and Other Writings* by Jack Kerouac. His recent book *Mill Power* documents the impact of a national park in Lowell, Massachusetts. His ancestors left France for North America in the 1600s, and their descendants settled in Lowell about 1880, both family lines having emigrated from Quebec to work in the robust textile-mill hub. Born in 1954 in Lowell, he grew up in a town nearby after the first suburban wave of the 1950s. He is a graduate of the University of Massachusetts in Lowell and studied in the creative writing program at the University of California in Irvine. For 40 years, he has been active in the transformation of Lowell from a struggling post-industrial city to the vital urban center of its region. His poems, essays, and articles have appeared in *Alaska Quarterly Review*, *The Massachusetts Review*, *Slate*, *The Christian Science Monitor*, *Carolina Quarterly*, *Aspect*, *Zone 3*, *Bohemian* (Japan), *Yankee*, and *The Salmon Literary Quarterly* (Ireland). His work is included in the anthologies *For a Living: The Poetry of Work*, *French Connections: A Gathering of Franco-American Poets*, and *Line Drives: 100 Contemporary Baseball Poems*. He lives with his family in Lowell.

BOOTSTRAP
PRESS